Advanced Praise for *Blazing New Ho*

"Clear, wise and personal, *Blazing New Homeschool Trails* encourages parents to help their teens find satisfying work through training in trades, job skills and life skills. Whether your teenager has developmental disabilities or just isn't cut out for college, this book will help you and your teen consider alternatives, customize your teens' education and equip them to contribute to their communities."

- Kathy Kuhl, homeschool coach, speaker and author of *Homeschooling Your Struggling Learner* and founder of www.learndifferently.com

"Whether you are a reluctant homeschool parent or an enthusiastic one, these tips will help you expand your journey and help you think through some avenues you might not have yet considered. There's even a list at the end to help you think through some key decisions in homeschooling. Instead of reading like an instructional manual, this resource weaves personal stories into the WHY behind exploring different avenues of learning and employment. Life experience and many hours of research make the authors experts on this topic, especially when similar resources just do not exist. Parents, therapists, and teachers will benefit from the journey of Natalie and Cindy with renewed passion to find the strengths in the students they teach instead of just focusing on the weaknesses and struggles. As a teacher and tutor, I highly recommend this resource!"

- Jennifer Donaldson, founder and educator at Tailor Joy www.tailorjoy.com

"I recommend this touching, heartfelt, and practical encouragement manual for parents of children who struggle with developmental issues. It feels like having a cup of coffee with friends while chatting about our children and our homeschooling journeys. How refreshing it is for experienced homeschooling mothers to offer reassurance that perfection is not our goal and education ought not to be a competition. This book is filled with resources and advice to help parents approach their children's future with realistic optimism and creativity."

- Lori Langdon, MD, FAAP, mom of six, adoptive mom, pediatrician, author, YouTube host, homeschool spouse

Advanced Praise for *Blazing New Homeschool Trails*

"Both Natalie Vecchione and Cindy LaJoy write from a place of such strength and good cheer about their homeschooling adventures in *Blazing New Homeschool Trails*, you're almost surprised to read about the self-doubt, roadblocks and frustrations they faced to get to their satisfied place. We're lucky they're so honest and detailed about their experiences in this engaging book about their own families. By the book's end, you'll come away with everything a parent needs to know about homeschooling as a way to help their neurodiverse child(ren) get the education *and life-experience* they need to learn, grow, and get on their feet as they head into adulthood. Having self-doubts about the commitment, resourcefulness and advocacy homeschooling takes to give your children what they need? Read this book. It will give you a roadmap and the confidence to take your first step. "

- Linda Rosenbaum, author of *Not Exactly As Planned: A Memoir About Love, Adoption and FASD*

"This book gives courage to those families who instinctively know that their children aren't truly understood in their current school situation but feel overwhelmed with the idea of homeschooling complex developmental disabilities. The authors suggested strategies focus on the child's strengths, accommodating weaknesses, cherishing the child for who they are, teaching with empathy and excitement, and enjoying the journey of daily discoveries where both parent and child are learning together. It celebrates the freedom to accommodate in a truly individualized manner rather than placing them in systems that have the potential to create more harm through inappropriate expectations and lack of support. This book gives the parent permission to slow down the pace and celebrate the goal of interdependence rather than striving for independence as modern society suggests is the only indicator of success. I so value the advice from parents who have completed this unique homeschooling journey before me and will be recommending this book to others as I know it fills a gap in the homeschooling community. "

- Leslie Jurado, Pediatric Occupational Therapist
  Co-Owner of Connected Kidz Pediatric Therapy
  www.connected-kidz.com

ENDORSEMENT for *Blazing New Homeschool Trails*

"As I read this book, I found myself saying, again and again, *Yes! So true! Perfectly said!* You see, even though I don't parent children with an FASD, developmental disability, or mental health diagnosis I am the oldest sibling of 14, 10 of whom have been added to my biological family through adoption and who have all struggled in similar ways to Cindy and Natalie's children. In fact, the stories and lessons that Cindy and Natalie share in this book were amazingly similar to those my parents have had to learn over their past 30 years as foster and adoptive parents, and why after I chose to homeschool my own children on the Autism Spectrum and they quickly followed suit and began their own homeschooling journey.

For this reason, without a shadow of a doubt, I know the wisdom these two women share in the following pages will not only educate you about your child, but will also provide you with resources you NEED to move forward in accepting and relating to the unique way your child requires support and compassion while navigating the path God has created for him or her to go by homeschooling through the teen years.

Thank you, Cindy and Natalie, for sharing your family's stories in a transparent yet informative way so other parents can face these same struggles with wisdom and understanding as they live out their calling to parent and home educate these very special children God has given them."

- Peggy Ployhar, Founder & CEO SPED Homeschool www.spedhomeschool.com

ENDORSEMENT for *Blazing New Homeschool Trails*

Great book with insights applicable far beyond homeschooling!

Cindy and Natalie provide readers with a first-hand experience of the power of "thinking brain", of the profound impact of meeting people where they are at, of accepting them for who they are, and of adjusting our expectations. While our society has traditionally been worried this has meant "giving up on people" or "not keeping them accountable", it is in fact the exact opposite. It is about acknowledging a different set of skills, focusing on individual strengths, supporting areas where, despite their very best effort, a person has significant challenges, and readjusting what "success" means for them.

Isn't that what we all want for ourselves and the people we love and care for? To be seen, heard, understood and supported? And when this happens, we take part in changing the trajectory of people's lives. Relationships are built and outcomes are improved for neurodiverse individuals who in the past, have been blamed for their invisible brain-based differences.

This goes against current values, beliefs and practices in our society, where tremendous efforts are being put on ensuring everyone meets similar expectations, at the cost of blaming and shunning people for their very real cognitive differences and making it difficult for them to develop confidence, self-esteem, and experience success.

Changing our ways is not easy, as Cindy and Natalie so honestly share, but it is the only way. It will get easier as people, services and organizations across our society in all systems in our society start understanding, recognizing and doing differently. It's about ***Trying Differently Rather than Harder***, as Diane Malbin, a trailblazer in the field of FASD and other brain-based conditions, so simply yet accurately summed it up almost 20 years ago.

Nathalie Brassard, Executive Director, FASCETS Inc.
https://fascets.org/

Blazing New Homeschool Trails

Natalie Vecchione
Cindy LaJoy

Blazing New Homeschool Trails

By Natalie Vecchione and Cindy LaJoy

© 2021 by Natalie Vecchione and Cindy LaJoy. All rights reserved. No part of this book may be reproduced, stored in a retrieval system or transmitted in any form or by any means- electronic, mechanical, recording, photocopy or otherwise- except for brief quotation for the purpose of commenting or review, with the prior permission of the authors / publishers.

Printed in the United States of America

Published by Natalie Vecchione and Cindy LaJoy

Scripture Quotations from The Holy Bible, New King James Version

Cover Design by Kerry Watson
www.iamkerrywatson.com/bookdesigns

Disclaimer –

We are not doctors, lawyers, mental health therapists or social workers. We do not provide legal or medical advice. All statements and views expressed are solely our opinion based on lived experiences or parent training. The content in this book is provided to families and professionals for information purposes only. It is not intended to replace professional medical, psychological, behavioral, legal, nutritional, or educational counsel. Reference to any specific books, materials, websites, programs, agencies, etc. is purely for informational purposes.

Natalie Vecchione – https://www.fasdhope.com

Cindy LaJoy – www.bluecollarhomeschool.com
https://www.buckaroosmontrose.com/

Blazing New Homeschool Trails –
https://www.blazingnewhomeschooltrails.com

About the authors –

Cindy LaJoy is the quintessential homeschool educator. When she homeschooled her five, internationally-adopted children (whose special needs ranged from FASD to exceptionally gifted), she was led to develop a "different kind of homeschool excellence" that she began at her table and developed into a 11.000+ member Facebook group, known as "Blue Collar Homeschool". This group, and its companion website (which is full of resources and links for families), provides families with the support she wished she had in her homeschool journey. Cindy combined her love of teaching, entrepreneurial spirit, training as a special needs academic advisor and job coach…and dreamed up "Buckaroos Slices and Scoops", which is a pizza and ice cream business specifically designed to accommodate the needs of her young adult children. Cindy hopes that through Buckaroos Slices and Scoops, her young adult children may not only survive in the employment world, but also one day may thrive as business owners. Of course, the mission of Buckaroos is also to hire other individuals with developmental disabilities and neurodiversity. Cindy's real-world experience in many areas has led her to: being a guest speaker on numerous podcasts, presenting at several regional homeschool conferences and being asked to contribute to three different books about special needs and homeschooling. Cindy's specialties include teaching and tutoring those with FASD, ADHD, Asperger's, Dyslexia, Dysgraphia, Dyscalculia, Reactive Attachment Disorder, Auditory / Visual Processing Disorders and Sensory Processing Disorder. Cindy offers special needs academic consulting and brainstorming for hands-on and project-based learning experiences. Cindy believes that learning is a life-long journey and she is currently pursuing ordination as an Interfaith Minister through One Spirit Seminary and she hopes to complete a course of study in Spiritual Counseling within the next three years.

About the authors -

Natalie Vecchione is an FASD parent advocate, homeschooler, podcast producer, podcast host, but most importantly….she is a mom! Natalie and her husband, John, grew their family through domestic adoption and they are the proud parents of a son and daughter. Prior to becoming a full-time homeschool mom, Natalie was a recreation and music therapist. Natalie received her undergraduate degree in Music Therapy from East Carolina University and her Masters of Therapeutic Recreation and Recreation Management from Florida International University. Natalie has been a Music Therapist-Board Certified for the past 25 years and she worked with the following populations: substance abuse, psychiatric, PTSD, geriatric, rehabilitation, early intervention and special needs. Natalie went from a career reinvention to a answering a calling as the result of their family's unique journey with Fetal Alcohol Spectrum Disorder (FASD). She has been a homeschool mom for over seven years. Natalie began advocating for FASD by being a FASD parent advocate, special needs homeschool parent mentor and peer support mentor. Natalie is certified in Mental Health First Aid and she has participated in several trainings about FASD. In 2019, she was honored to be chosen as one of fifty parents in the state of North Carolina to participate in the first ECAC Parent Leadership Summit. In 2020, Natalie and John co-founded FASD Hope. Natalie produces and hosts the FASD Hope podcast series. FASD Hope's mission is to provide awareness, information and inspiration for people whose lives have been touched by FASD.

ACKNOWLEDGEMENTS-

From Natalie - I give all praise and glory to my Lord and Savior, Jesus Christ, for my salvation and giving me the GRACE and discernment on this journey of being a wife and mom! Thank you to the friends and my family members who have supported our family on our unique journey. Thank you to Cindy LaJoy for inspiring me and encouraging me to take a leap of faith in this journey! Thank you to the FASD, Special Needs Homeschool Mama Warriors (you know who you are) for being my tribe! Thank you to Rev. Dr. Candi Asheden for your amazing insight and feedback in helping us edit this book! Many thanks to our Book Launch Team for their awesome support, feedback and encouragement. Lastly, I couldn't have embarked on this adventure without the love and support of my husband, John and our amazing kids, Nick and Gianna…I love you!

From Cindy –

The greatest teachers impact our lives in powerful ways and I have been incredibly blessed to have amazing teachers along the way, with our five kids having taught me more than anyone else in my life. Matthew, Kenny, Joshua, Angela, and Olesya- you are my treasures. I have always dubbed us as "The Family That God Built" and nothing could be truer. My husband, Dominick, has opted in with great enthusiasm to any crazy idea I have come up with and I am profoundly grateful for his trust and confidence in me. I am thankful for numerous individuals who invested a great deal in our family, sharing their gifts and even financial support to ensure we succeeded against all odds. Thank you to the literally thousands of parents, through the past 20 years, who have shared their stories on Yahoo and Facebook groups and allowed me to gain wisdom from reading of their experiences. A special thanks to Rev. Dr. Candi Ashenden, our editor and my truest, dearest friend. I am better because of your friendship. Finally, a great big thank you to Natalie Vecchione for her prodding me to share some of what I have learned, her enthusiastic tackling of all the details and in bringing our guidebook to fruition.

DEDICATION –

Cindy and Natalie would like to dedicate this book to our families –

The LaJoy Family and The Vecchione Family for your love, support and inspiration. You all are the reason we blaze these new trails!

Finally, Cindy and Natale would like to dedicate this book to all of the families of children / teens / young adults with Fetal Alcohol Spectrum Disorders and other Developmental Disabilities and who are advocating, supporting and trying figuring it out as you go along. This book was written for you!

CONTENTS

Introduction   1

Preface   4

Chapter 1
Cindy's Journey as a Homeschool Mom   10

Chapter 2
Blue Collar Homeschool and

Buckaroos Slices and Scoops   20

Chapter 3
Natalie's Journey as a Homeschool Mom   32

Chapter 4
Homeschool Trade School   45

Chapter 5
Tips and Tools for Homeschooling Teens with Developmental Disabilities   61

CONTENTS

Chapter 6

"A-Ha!" Moments and Finding Support   71

Chapter 7

Blazing New Trails   77

Chapter 8
Embracing Interdependence   83

Chapter 9

Reflections for the Weary Homeschool Parent   89

Chapter 10

Moving Forward   93

INTRODUCTION

From Natalie -

    Cindy and I are writing this book as a guide for homeschool families of children, teens, and young adults who learn differently. We have joked that <u>this book</u> is the one we wish we had about five to seven years ago! Cindy and I both chose to homeschool our respective families because we wanted our children (now young adults) to have the best possibility of living fulfilling lives that would bring them a sense of accomplishment and joy. When there weren't many options for the future of our children, we decided to <u>create</u> new options and opportunities. Living a different kind of life doesn't necessarily mean a *less than* kind of life.

    Perhaps your child has a developmental disability or a neurodiversity...or just learns and interacts with his or her world in a way that is different. Your child may be on a path that does not include post-homeschooling academia and we have learned from our respective, lived experiences that this can be a confusing, isolating, and uncertain journey. You may be asking *What are my teen's unique gifts and skills?* or *What will my teen do once homeschool is over?* Years ago, Cindy and I were each faced with these questions. With both of us having teens diagnosed with Fetal Alcohol Spectrum Disorders (FASDs), Cindy and I (separately, yet at the same time) had decisions to make about our teens' futures.

    How would we homeschool our teens, knowing that they would not pursue college, university, or even trade school after homeschool? REINVENTION! Both Cindy and I, in our respective homeschool journeys, learned that if no current paths were going to work for our teens (who had many strengths that the world needed to learn about), then we would BLAZE NEW HOMESCHOOL TRAILS for our teens' futures. As homeschool moms of teens who learned differently, we needed to reinvent our teens' homeschool journeys to best prepare them for their futures.

Cindy created the "Blue Collar Homeschool" website and the 11,000 plus member "Blue Collar Homeschool" Facebook page. Her family's *homeschool finale* involved a year-long journey of creating the award-winning "Buckaroos Slices and Scoops" Pizza and Ice Cream Restaurant in Montrose, Colorado.

At the same time, across the United States in North Carolina, I was learning how to network with skilled woodworkers and carpenters to create an *old-fashioned, one-to-one apprenticeship* for our son's newfound gift of woodworking and carpentry. On a very small scale, with two incredibly talented and kind carpenters, we developed a *Homeschool Trade School* for our son.

Cindy and I quickly learned that our teens had many talents and we were blessed to be the *Treasure Finders* in discovering the gifts of our teens and how we, as homeschool moms, could help them blaze new trails for their lives *after homeschool*. This book is for all of you homeschool families of kids, teens, and young adults who learn differently...just like ours. We are sharing our journeys for you parents who are *uncertain* about the years after homeschool. **THIS** is the handbook, the guidebook, and the story of journeys that **WE** wished we had known about as our children approached their teens! Despite the diagnoses of your child / teen / young adult, there lie gifts and strengths within them…and it is *your* responsibility to discover those gifts and strengths! It is time to create new ways for your kids to learn and to think **out of the box** about their futures! Are you ready to blaze new homeschool trails for your families?! Great!! Then here we go…

PREFACE

A Refresher Course in Fetal Alcohol Spectrum Disorder (FASD)

and Developmental Disabilities

From Natalie-

We know that many of the homeschool parents reading this book have chosen the homeschooling path of learning for their child because their child *learns differently* or because they want their children to develop their gifts and talents. Cindy and I understand, as moms of young adults who learn differently, that the homeschooling lifestyle gives parents the ability to nurture their child's strengths...while supporting their needs. We chose homeschooling for the same reasons and discovered new reasons to keep on homeschooling during those challenging days! As we've previously stated, this book is the guide we wish we could have read when our young adults, who had Fetal Alcohol Spectrum Disorders (FASDs), were trying to figure out their gifts in the midst of their challenges. Before we begin sharing our journeys and experiences, Cindy and I want to share some important information about developmental disabilities, including Fetal Alcohol Spectrum Disorder (FASD), and the reasons and motivations behind our blazing different paths for the futures of our young adults' lives.

The Centers for Disease Control (CDC) defines developmental disabilities as "a group of conditions due to an impairment in physical, learning, language, or behavior areas". Having a developmental disability affects an individual's daily functioning and a developmental disability is a life-long condition. Some examples of developmental disabilities include (but are not limited to) the following: Attention Deficit / Hyperactivity Disorder (ADD / ADHD), Autism Spectrum Disorder (ASD), Cerebral Palsy, Fetal Alcohol Spectrum Disorder (FASD), Fragile X Syndrome, Intellectual Disabilities (IDD) and Learning Disorders*. Most developmental disabilities have a mix of causes or unknown causes. Many developmental disabilities are also hereditary and there are a number of risk factors that can contribute to a child having a developmental disability, including maternal infections, premature birth, untreated or late treatment of jaundice and prenatal exposure to alcohol.

Developmental Disabilities result in impairments in several or more of the following domains of life functioning: mobility, self-care, receptive and expressive language, learning, following directions, capacity for living independently, adaptive functioning and financial independence. Although developmental disabilities are life-long disabilities, early diagnosis, early intervention, and a supportive environment with accommodations can have a significant impact on a child's ability to learn and acquire skills.

FASD is a **brain-based disability** with whole-body symptoms. The disabilities that are caused by prenatal alcohol exposure fall under the umbrella of FASD. A common misconception about FASD is that an individual must have the "facial characteristics" or outward physical characteristics associated with Fetal Alcohol Syndrome in order to have a Fetal Alcohol Spectrum Disorder. Fetal Alcohol Syndrome (FAS) is **one** of several diagnoses under the FASD Diagnosis Umbrella. Most people recognize the facial characteristics that accompany Fetal Alcohol Syndrome (FAS), such as smooth philtrum, thin upper lip, and short palpebral fissure lengths. However, it is important to note that those facial characteristics associated with FAS only form between days 17-23 of gestation. Therefore, if an unborn child is prenatally exposed to alcohol any time before or after that time frame, that unborn child will have an FASD, but may not have any of the facial characteristics associated with prenatal alcohol exposure. As a result, approximately 90% of those individuals with an FASD **do not** have facial characteristics associated with prenatal alcohol exposure.***

Another important statistic to note is that over 400 medical diagnoses / conditions can occur with Fetal Alcohol Spectrum Disorders. Not only does prenatal alcohol exposure affect the brain of an unborn child, it can affect nearly every system of the body. Cindy and I saw firsthand how prenatal alcohol exposure affected our children's bodies through their birth defects, cardiovascular, respiratory, endocrine, gastrointestinal, and autoimmune diagnoses and challenges.

Despite of being the most misdiagnosed, underdiagnosed and undiagnosed of the developmental disabilities, Fetal Alcohol Spectrum Disorder (FASD) is the leading cause of developmental disabilities in the Western World (source: fascets.org). A 2018 Study, published in the Journal of the American Medical Association (JAMA) and led by Phillip May, Ph.D. from University of North Carolina – Chapel Hill estimated the prevalence of FASD among first graders in US communities to be up to 1 in 20****. Yet, despite the increasing research about FASD, approximately 90% of those with an FASD are misdiagnosed or undiagnosed. FASD is *more prevalent* than people realize and FASD is a significant social and public health crisis in our country (and in the world). As moms of young adults with FASD, Cindy and I know first-hand that actions that are commonly mistaken as "behaviors" are actually symptoms of FASD.

Some of the Primary Behavioral Characteristics of FASD include:

- Dysmaturity or being socially developmentally younger than an individual's chronological age
- Impulsivity
- Distractibility
- Slower Processing Pace
- Difficulty with Memory, Problems with Working Memory, Inconsistent Performance
- Difficulty with Abstract Thinking
- Difficulty with Cause and Effect
- Sensory Overstimulation or Sensory Sensitivity

   (Source "Trying Differently Rather Than Harder" by Diane Malbin MSW, Tectrice, Inc. (Portland, OR ; 1999/2017).

Cindy and I learned, the hard way, that there needs to be a paradigm shift in thinking. We need to move from thinking a child *won't* do something to realizing when a child *can't* do something. When an individual has an FASD diagnosis, it is imperative for parents / caregivers / loved ones to understand that FASD is a **brain-based disability** with whole-body symptoms. We cannot change the brains of our children, but we *can* accommodate, meet them where they're at, adapt learning strategies / styles / support needs and **focus on strengths.** This book will explain how we homeschooled our teens/young adults who learned differently, while helping them discover and nurture their strengths to prepare them for life beyond homeschool. Most importantly, we want to share hope. Your family's homeschool path may look different from the paths of those with typically developing children / teens, but it doesn't mean it has to be a *less than* path! Although we have experienced (and continue to experience) challenging times, our respective families have also been blessed to enjoy unique celebrations and victories that come when young adults who experience the world on a different path succeed.

Listed below are some FASD Specific Resources for more information. You can also find resources our website https://www.fasdhope.com

FASD Homepage on CDC- https://www.cdc.gov/ncbddd/fasd/index.html

FASCETS (Fetal Alcohol Spectrum Consultation and Education Training Services)

https://fascets.org/

"Trying Differently Rather Than Harder: Fetal Alcohol Spectrum Disorders" by Diane Malbin, MSW (1999/2002/2017), FASCETS, Inc. Tectrice, Inc. (Portland, OR).

NOFAS https://www.nofas.org/

Proof Alliance https://www.proofalliance.org/

Canada FASD Research Network https://www.canfasd.ca/

NOFASD – Australia https://www.nofasd.org.au/

References-

*****Centers for Disease Control and Prevention**
https://www.cdc.gov/

******FASCETS – Fetal Alcohol Spectrum Consultation Education and Training Services** https://fascets.org/

*******FASCETS**

********May, et al. "Prevalence of Fetal Alcohol Spectrum Disorders in 4 US Communities. JAMA. 2018;319(5):474-482.**

Chapter 1

Cindy's Journey as a Homeschool Mom

Having no intent to homeschool when their children were preschool aged, many parents later describe themselves as "Accidental Homeschoolers", because somewhere along the line something went wrong for their children with the traditional public-school model and they fell into homeschooling as an alternative. What a lovely thought, as if there were choices to be made and this was yet another to be explored! When asked why we began homeschooling, I have always explained that we were "Desperation Homeschoolers", being too poor to afford private school or tutors for five children, and knowing we were going to have a nightmare on our hands if we continued with a system that simply was not set up to handle the diverse needs of five internationally adopted, experientially deprived learners, three of whom came to us as older adoptees at ages 8, 10 and almost 12 years old, and two of whom came to us as infants who were far outpacing their public school peers due to giftedness. Our leap into homeschooling smelled of fear and looked like panic, rather than appearing to be the sweet little experience of trying an alternative to see if we might happen to like it better.

It began on the first day of 5th grade for our son, Matt, who had always eagerly anticipated each new school year and loved learning. Adopted from an orphanage in Aktobe, Kazakhstan at 11 months old, he was a quiet, reserved, bright boy who seemed to drink deeply of anything that was history-oriented. He came home after that first afternoon and trudged down the hall toward his bedroom dragging his backpack behind him after quietly declaring this was going to be the longest year of his life. What? Why? What happened? We soon realized that the majority of his class was reading two grades below grade level, and with Matt's 10th grade reading level in 5th grade, the gap was just too large for him to be engaged any longer. After a morning of volunteering in his classroom, it was easy to see this was no longer going to work for him, and we needed to make a change. Observing him in class, I saw something disturbing. The slouch with which he sat, his head occasionally resting on the desk as he patiently waited ten minutes for the class to define the word "agreement", and the unusual antsy behavior that he exhibited, told me all I needed to know. I left his school that day and called my husband, Dominick, as I walked out the door telling him, "I know this seems drastic, but my gut is telling me we are going to lose him, or at the very least his spirit, if we don't get him out of here, and I mean NOW." That night we had a long conversation about alternatives, and felt we had few options but to consider homeschooling, something I desperately didn't want to do.

Little did I know how powerfully life-changing this decision would be for our kids, and also for me!

Sitting down with Matt, I asked how he felt about the idea of homeschooling. I was encouraged when I saw he was quite open to the idea, but neither of us could envision what it might entail nor what it would look like. We talked through the pros and cons, and together we came to the conclusion that we should give it a try, even if only for the remainder of his 5th grade year.

Fortunately, this was an opportune time to try homeschooling, as we already knew that his school year was going to be interrupted when our entire family traveled to Petropavlovsk, Kazakhstan to add Olesya and Angela (biological sisters who were 10 and almost 12 years old) to our family. Matt would be joined by his two brothers on this trip, Joshua, who was then six years old and in 1st grade and had been adopted at 11 months old from Uralsk, Kazakhstan, and Kenny, who had joined our family three years earlier from an orphanage in Bishkek, Kyrgyzstan as an 8-year-old. Then 11 years old and in 4th grade, Kenny's seeming inability to learn how to read, and his overall academic struggles that the school blamed on being an English Language Learner was also causing growing concern. We had already half-heartedly considered withdrawing Kenny for a year from public school to see if having some intense one-on-one instruction would help him gain ground. We were soon going to learn that there was much more to Kenny's challenges...

After a week of research, Matt and I sat outside his school, both of us dreading having to walk through those doors and explain that we were disenrolling him. We loved his school and the staff there, who had been incredibly kind and supportive of us through the past five years. We knew that we were embarking on an unusual journey that might last a single year, or eight years, but at the time so much was unknown to us and we were both apprehensive, yet committed to giving homeschooling a try. Taking a deep breath and grabbing hold of each other's hands, we marched through the doors and into a new way of life.

The next day, we sat across the kitchen table from one another, and I admitted I had a lot to learn about how to do this, and needed more time to pull together a cohesive plan, but I asked Matt what he was interested in learning about if he had a choice. His response? The Cold War and the Cuban Missile Crisis. I swallowed hard, tried not to be intimidated by that response, and realized this was the perfect example of why our son didn't fit in academically with his 5th grade peers, and was the very reason why we were giving homeschooling a try! Thankfully, a wonderful friend jumped at the chance to teach a course on these subjects to Matt while I spent a few weeks cramming, studying, and researching everything I could about putting together a 5th grade course of study. We rediscovered the library, a place that was one of our favorite haunts when he was pre-school aged, but his love of reading had slowly diminished with assigned reading in class and he now seldom read much for fun. I will never forget that first week when we stood among the shelves quietly talking and I was encouraging him to find something to read. He looked at me and asked, "Well Mom, what are you assigning me to read?" and I replied, "I am not assigning you anything! Grab as many books as you want on any topic that interests you. Come on, you know how to do this!" The grin that slowly spread across his face told me everything I needed to know, and thus began the days of multiple laundry baskets filled with books on all kinds of subjects being hauled back and forth. He later told me, "I forgot how much I like reading! Thanks for letting me pick out books I actually like." How telling that was about how the system can systematically relegate reading to drudgery rather than joy!

In early December of 2010, we boarded the plane in our little hometown of Montrose, Colorado to begin the long, yet now familiar journey halfway across the globe to finally embrace our daughters. Among all our luggage was a suitcase filled to the brim with schoolwork for all three of our sons, two of whom had been provided with folders of worksheets in math, reading, and writing, along with many age-appropriate books. We also had all of Matt's schoolwork as well, assigned by his new, inexperienced teacher. Planning to be overseas for two weeks, we felt well prepared and knew our sons would return having had a unique adventure as well as on target with all of their assigned work. The best laid plans usually fall apart to remind us of how little control we actually have, and this trip was no exception. Due to circumstances beyond our control, two weeks turned into two and a half months in Southern Siberia as the adoption process became more complicated and required additional time in the country.

However, it was during this time that I had an unwanted, yet very necessary epiphany. Two separate experiences spoke loudly into my life, challenging me to accept something I vehemently wanted to reject, and yet knowing if I said "Yes" to God on this, only good would come of it even if I couldn't yet see it.

The first sign that would change the course of our life came when working with Kenny while we were settled in our cozy apartment as the bitter winds chilled the air outside to as cold as -65 degrees. That same chill was felt inside as we quickly discovered that Kenny's learning challenges had little to do with learning English and everything to do with a seemingly faulty memory and a complete lack of critical thinking. We had, of course, sensed things were not quite normal for Kenny, but given his background and lack of exposure to the world at large due to his being institutionalized since birth, we didn't have the ability to discern earlier how many of his difficulties were due to his prior life, how much was due to language acquisition, or if something else was in the mix. Being a child with a bilateral cleft and lip, speech issues were also in the mix for Kenny.

It was in reading aloud to him one night that my husband and I both had a wake-up call. Hearing the story of Laura Ingalls Wilder's *Little House in the Big Woods*, Kenny asked what a butter churn was, so I explained it to him. It appeared three more times while we read that night, and each time Kenny had to ask again what it was. Frustrated, I told him I had already explained what it was multiple times, and I accused him of not paying attention. This sweet little boy was almost inconsolable when in anguish he cried out, "I *am* trying to remember, Mommy, but I can't! I am sorry!! I really am trying!" Later, I called my husband into our bedroom and explained to him that I was now certain there was something truly wrong with our son, and it had nothing to do with learning English. Things didn't make sense to him and he retained very little of what was presented to him even when it was presented slowly and clearly and multiple times.

That night I paced the floor, unable to sleep. I knew what I had to do. I knew what God was asking of me, but how I struggled with obedience on this! It was becoming ever clearer that I had a choice to make, and I didn't like any of the options.

In visiting our daughters daily prior to finalizing their adoptions, their lack of foundational knowledge was growing apparent. Despite knowing there was an entire ocean that separated the continents we were being asked unusual questions such as if we were driving all the way to America. Angela, then almost 12 years old, asked if, once we were home, we could go see the mermaids when we were home because she thought they were real. Both girls struggled to understand the differences between fiction or true stories on TV, and they had never been exposed to many of the things we take for granted that a kindergartener knows, such as what was a bank, what happened at a post office, how to shop in a store, and much more. I couldn't begin to imagine how this incredible lack of knowledge combined with the naiveté they both exhibited would cause them to be taken advantage of in public middle school.

Prior to leaving for Kazakhstan, Josh's 1st grade teacher had also already pulled me aside, saying she had heard we had decided to pull Matt from school and wondered if we had any plans to homeschool Josh as well. Laughing, I had told her that I had my hands full just trying to figure it all out for one child, and we had no long-term plans yet at all. Hesitating, she then shared that I might want to consider homeschooling Josh as well, for she could already see he was well ahead of his peers and she feared that by 3rd grade we might be facing the same situation with Josh that we had experienced with Matt.

Though that conversation unsettled me, I brushed it off as I had many other things on my mind and no intention of becoming a permanent full-time homeschooler. Fast forward to that night in Kazakhstan, tears streaming down as my heart screamed out, "NOOOOO!!! I don't want this kind of responsibility and I don't even know HOW to do this! Really God? REALLY?? You want me to teach English to two brand new children of ours, teach at a gifted level for at least one who is interested in things I have no clue about, and somehow figure out how to help Kenny while also making sure Josh isn't somehow left behind?" I had never been more terrified or overwhelmed with begrudging certainty. It was as if I could see into the future and could envision our family five years down the road with the kids all well into the teen years, still attending public school, and the entire family collapsing under the weight of poor decisions made earlier on. I knew what my kids needed, and it was clear I was getting signs from every corner that pointed me in the right direction. All I had to do was say "Yes", but in many ways, it felt like dying to self in a way that had never been asked of me before, and I honestly didn't think I had it in me. Of course, the love I felt for our five kids won, and after battling God all night I told Dominick the next morning that I had come to the conclusion that we were going to jump fully into homeschooling, that I was absolutely certain that this was the right thing to do for them, though I wasn't so sure if it was the right thing to do for myself. That was all it took for him to agree and thank me for being willing, while he also promised to put his all into finding a way to make it financially feasible for me to remain home to tackle homeschooling.

Saying "Yes" when the Holy Spirit asks us to do something we inwardly kick and scream over is perhaps the hardest thing to do, and yet the rewards that come are often an unexpected gift!

The first three years were a blur. As I gained my sea legs with homeschooling, I was shocked to discover I was actually a creative and patient teacher who grew to thoroughly enjoy homeschooling! Gradually gaining confidence and insisting on all of us treating this process with great diligence, I couldn't have asked for more eager, enthusiastic, dedicated students. Beginning at preschool level for some topics while stretching toward high school with some subjects with Matt in middle school, we found our way. I discovered I was a natural Socratic-style educator, and an avid researcher, and I began to weave my way through various learning disabilities, diagnoses, and accommodations.

Together, we created a structured learning environment and explored everything, allowing space in our schedule to follow rabbit trails, Googling everything from what does a thatched roof look like to how old muskets fired. I learned to present things visually, or hands-on as often as possible, to enhance retention for our three who have Fetal Alcohol Spectrum Disorder. We also learned to accommodate slow processing speeds and twice exceptionalism with Matt who was diagnosed with giftedness along with Dysgraphia. Olesya struggled with Dyscalculia, Kenny needed ongoing speech therapy, and also was discovered to suffer significantly with Auditory Processing Disorder. Oh yes, then we were also continuing to teach a new language with English!

Homeschooling allowed for success and real-life learning that never would have been possible in public school classrooms. Using project-based learning, the entire family renovated a repossessed modular home, purchased solely for the experience we could offer the kids, who did all the work including drywall repair, minor plumbing and electrical work, painting the interior, laying flooring, and even interviewing potential renters! Other projects included: a year-long documentary filmed and edited by Josh, the designing and building of a custom 3D printer by Matt who also became a pilot at 19 years old and culminated in the development of a business to be run after graduation by Olesya, Angela, and Kenny! With the freedom to teach to each individual learners' level, we were able to help them soar. Each of our kids graduated reading and writing at a 12th grade level, and though still struggling from time to time with deficits, our three with FASD have a very positive outlook on life. All three are moving into adulthood in a healthy manner, even if more slowly than their same age peers, and we have thankfully experienced none of the typical behavioral challenges inherent with FASD. With rock solid family relationships each of our young adults was well prepared to enter the world.

And I grew as well...in totally unexpected ways. My "patience muscle" grew to be far stronger than I ever would have envisioned it could be. I developed skills teaching those with learning challenges and now I work as an educator with other students who need an instructor who believes in them and has the patience to offer a slower learning pace and the repetition necessary for success. I unexpectedly blossomed into someone I had no idea dwelled beneath the surface. Perhaps the most surprising thing was how the "Desperation Homeschooler" evolved into the "Enthusiastic Homeschooler"!

Chapter 2

Blue Collar Homeschool and Buckaroos Slices and Scoops

From Cindy-

"Desperation Homeschooling" led to many unexpected joys around our kitchen table, and it also led to finding new ways to meet our family's needs. Prior to this point in my life I had never seen the more resourceful side of myself. However, as the saying goes, "A worried mom does better research than the FBI" and nothing could be truer! So, what do you do when all your research plants you firmly at a dead end, when you discover there are very few resources available? What do you do when there is no safe place to share your concerns and find experienced mentors to guide you? You create it!

Blue Collar Homeschool was born, once again, out of desperation. I was lonely, lost in my homeschooling journey, because there was almost no one in my day-to-day life who understood all of what our family was going through. The challenges were enormous, the sheer volume of special needs I was dealing with every single day was disheartening, and there seemed to be nowhere safe to turn. Friends tried to understand and many offered concrete assistance by tutoring, taking the kids on the occasional field trip, and some even helped financially. However, no one truly understood how overwhelmed I felt every single day as I sat before my beautiful brood and felt the weight of their futures resting heavily upon my shoulders. As learning disabilities began to become more obvious and could no longer be blamed solely on language acquisition, I became not only their teacher, but the special needs evaluator and advocate for services, the therapist, the curriculum planner, and much more. The laundry list of special needs was well beyond the norm: Reactive Attachment Disorder, Dysgraphia, Dyscalculia, English as a Second Language, Sensory Integration Disorder, Auditory Processing Disorder, Fetal Alcohol Spectrum Disorder, stuttering, speech and language delays, processing speed deficits, short and long-term memory loss, giftedness, and much more were all part of our daily lives. Add in the frequent out-of-state visits to Shriners Hospitals for ongoing cleft lip and palate surgeries for one son, ongoing painful back issues leading ultimately to spinal fusion surgery for another son, facilitating the healing from trauma and neglect, and it was all incredibly overwhelming. Where could I turn for support and ideas?

Sadly, it seemed that even in online homeschooling groups our reality was judged or dismissed. I never dared share too much as I had already witnessed far too many special needs parents being criticized for not teaching algebra, for adapting curriculum as necessary, or for not preparing their child well enough for college. College?! Are you kidding me?!! I was panicking over my 12-year-old being unable to read at a first-grade level! College wasn't even on the radar for some of our kids, particularly in those early years. I was knee deep in trying to help some of our kids think logically about such simple things as where frozen meat is stored (hint: not in the pantry), that frosting is used to decorate a cake (hint: not gravy), and that toilet paper goes in the toilet (hint: not in the trash can as in your birth country!) The last thing I needed was someone judging me for a situation that was impossible for them to understand.

Consequently, I spent many years of our homeschooling journey feeling somewhat isolated, disheartened, and like an utter failure despite doing my very best to educate our kids and meet their many needs. Perhaps it was the desperation I felt in those early years and the frustration of slogging my way through until I finally began to see some light at the end of the tunnel that compelled me to create the Blue Collar Homeschool website and Facebook group. I knew there had to be other moms out there who were discouraged and feeling every bit the failure because their child wasn't performing at the level others were. I knew there had to be moms who, even if their child had no special needs, were also feeling like they weren't doing enough because their child was simply not academically inclined and had no interest in attending college. Where was the hope for these families? Where was the encouragement? What resources were available for the very average or below average learner? How could I walk alongside them on their journey to alleviate some of the despair and loneliness?

Blue Collar Homeschool (BCH) may have been born out of desperation, but it became a place of incredible inspiration for thousands of homeschoolers! As the founder of BCH, I established that this was going to be the safe place I had always needed, and we were going to share about "A different kind of homeschooling excellence!". We are a group that is purposeful in the pursuit of an education that is appropriate for our particular children, thoughtful with our responses, and helpful in recommending resources previously unknown to others. We celebrate the unusual triumphs…the teen who finally masters writing a five-paragraph essay, the youngster who starts their own dog walking business, or the girl who sells her first painting. We share photos of trucks that have been rebuilt, barns that have been raised, and cakes that have been baked. Along the way, we also share resources ranging from Math for Excavating, to apprenticeship opportunities, to farrier schools. Most importantly, our Facebook group is there, day or night, when one of us is feeling low, when failure seeps in around the edges, when judgment from outside has done some damage within. We commiserate, we collaborate and we rejuvenate. We help each other clarify our focus, so we can get back to teaching our kids by meeting them where they are at, not where we wish we thought they should be. Blue Collar Homeschool has been the emotional salvation for so many families who now have a safe space to share their reality, their struggles, and their triumphs even if that reality, struggle, and triumph wouldn't be viewed as such in many circles.

In my family, our old friend Desperation began to creep in as we closed in on graduation for our three with FASD. It was obvious that remaining employed in a traditional setting would be a real challenge, given their memory issues and many learning disabilities. However, in an adapted environment they were experiencing great success! All three were reading and writing at a 12th grade level, they had become well versed in history and government, and Kenny even managed to handle Pre-Calculus! However, science eluded them, driving was still out of reach for all three (though by age 21, two managed to obtain their licenses), advanced math for our daughters was out of the question and brain function was spotty and depended on the day.

Since each one brought true gifts that could benefit any employer, there was no doubt about their ability to obtain employment, only to maintain it. Through no fault of their own, these three who had overcome so much were going to be hard-pressed to find the right work setting in which they could thrive. Angela had already attempted job training a year earlier to become a home health aide and though there is no doubt she could have performed the job well (and indeed was already assisting a family friend's aging mom), she simply couldn't learn the same way as others and was overwhelmed on day two of her training, returning home in tears and deciding that she would not be able to continue.

As graduation loomed at ages 20 and 21 for our three, Dominick and I knew we might have no choice but to find some way to employ them ourselves. At the very least, they needed a couple of years of full-time protected employment in order to learn customer service skills and perhaps other transferable experience. They would ultimately always need an employer who would understand their randomness of brain function, and wouldn't be angry if a task they had mastered yesterday was not remembered a week later.

The summer before their senior year, I began to have the glimmer of an idea. Spending two weeks in New England, I saw first-hand the popularity of dairy bars (ice cream stands for those not familiar) and wondered if a business as simple as ice cream sales would be possible. After some investigation and consideration of what might be partnered with ice cream that also would be reasonably uncomplicated to make, the idea for Buckaroos Slices and Scoops emerged. We presented the idea of a pizza and ice cream business to the kids to see what they thought about working together in their own business. We pointed out how their gifts and weaknesses dovetailed beautifully, with some being stronger in areas the others were weaker, and how together, all three of them made a wonderful team and might be able to manage their own restaurant! Knowing we had spare space located inside the business my husband owned in a high traffic location, and recognizing that pizza and ice cream had all the ingredients right in front of them which simplified preparation, this seemed to be something that was fully possible. They all heartily agreed, and so we embarked on a year-long adventure to help our kids become entrepreneurs!

      This was a capstone project unlike any other. Putting their year of entrepreneurship classes to great use, they spent their senior year crafting a business plan, learning all about quality levels of ice cream, and creating a budget. We attended the International Pizza Expo where they attended seminars and visited with over 500 vendors as they wandered the showroom floor. In sampling everything from toasted ravioli to individual sauces, their excitement grew. It was here at this event that I witnessed them each stand a little taller as they engaged in important conversations, asked pertinent questions, and saw they were being taken seriously by those they interacted with. How could one not take a very young person seriously when he or she stands before you asking questions about liability limits for insurance, comparing and contrasting the quality of various crusts, and speaking intelligently about the merits of particular ovens. They may have been rookies, but they were well-prepared rookies!

      Josh and Matt were also part of the process, contributing their substantial gifts to their siblings' endeavors. Matt, a budding website developer, created the Buckaroos web site and assisted occasionally on site with construction. In addition to being a full-time student, Josh also spent many hours building walls, helping in myriad ways, and later becoming an employee of Buckaroos.

      While Dominick oversaw the construction and the kids provided much of the labor, I was helping the kids envision their future as they crafted a mission statement, learned about social media advertising, examined balance sheets and profit and loss statements as they learned more about accounting, and crafted everything from employee handbooks to biographies and menus. Their plan was to employ others like themselves who might struggle to gain a foothold in the employment world, so they decided to hire employees with developmental and/or cognitive delays who might be able to use their experience at Buckaroos as a stepping stone to eventual higher paying jobs.

What a learning experience this was for our emerging young adults! Learning to adapt, overcome, and accommodate, the business gradually began to take shape. How I admired their energy and work ethic, as they spent ten to twelve hours a day involved in everything from tearing down concrete block walls, painting, laying new flooring and much more!

The physical work required was no small amount, but the intellectual work required just as much attention. Using a poster board, we laid out the entire store with a one foot to one inch ratio to make the math simpler for our daughter with Dyscalculia. Cut outs to represent each piece of equipment, the counter, and the seating area and countless hours were spent moving pieces around until we found the perfect fit for our small space. It was determined that one of them would take the manager level of the required ServSafe food safety training, and Olesya studied hard for that, passing on her very first attempt! All of our kids had previous experience working in a little café we had owned in their younger years, so they had a foundation to build on in food service. Kenny worked alongside our young friend, Billy, a college student at USC who interned with us that summer who learned new skills himself. Kenny and Billy were the perfect team to analyze food costs and come up with profitable price points for every single menu item. Listening to them debate the cost versus quality concerns on everything from disposable cups to cheese was an educational experience for me!

We saw such incredible growth during the year of business development. Each of the kids gained confidence as they began speaking on their own behalf with various local vendors and officials. Interacting with insurance agents, the health inspector, computer specialists, and other professionals provided important experience. I planned to be present working alongside them for a year or two until they felt solid enough to fly on their own. They were rapidly maturing, and it was affirming for me in all kinds of ways to see their progress, and how they were building on prior knowledge that had taken so much effort to instill! Writing took on new meaning when used in real life to reach out to a beverage distributor asking for samples and equipment costs. Math had real life consequences when calculations were done incorrectly, and reading the fine print of every contract and insurance policy became crucial. Quickly, they discovered that understanding the details of a legal document meant the difference between them being treated as a rookie or being viewed as knowledgeable enough that they couldn't easily be taken advantage of. Hearing from our insurance agent how Billy and Kenny had asked better questions than almost any other adult coming in for a commercial policy had me glowing with pride!

Hiring others, training them and finding ways to adapt the environment for the highest possibility of success were important tasks. We needed a strong support staff of traditional employees who also had innate compassion and inordinate patience. We were blessed to have just the right people walk through the door looking for work, and the team started taking shape. Posting laminated instructions and visuals everywhere possible and doing a lot of hands-on training before ever opening the doors was an important strategy. Our two "soft opening" evenings with friends and family who came in to be practice customers revealed to us where we needed to tweak processes. It felt like every member of our church attended, driving an hour each way to be helpful and celebrate with us!

We opened the doors on October 15, 2019, five months before a global pandemic arrived. In December 2019, it became obvious that our kids were well prepared to take over, and my presence was no longer needed, much to our delight. In fact, my presence proved to be a hindrance, as everyone wanted to turn to the adult in the room rather than view our three as managers. I bowed out and turned it all over to the kids, who proceeded to do a fabulous job of running Buckaroos! Every new business needs a mentor, and my husband and I have now moved into that role. The day-to-day operation is handled solely by Kenny, Angela, and Olesya, who have even had occasion to have to gently reprimand employees, handle cash deficits and problem-solve the repair of equipment. They have created a lovely and compassionate community with their employees and Buckaroos Slices and Scoops was even voted "Best in the Valley" in both the pizza and ice cream category in their first year!

What are they still struggling with? They will never be able to fully handle the accounting pieces all on their own, though Kenny is quite sharp in this area and does understand it all, but his executive functioning issues get in the way. We have already had a two-week period after a minor medical procedure for Olesya in which she was given one dose of a narcotic and her brain function was greatly impacted, necessitating her being off the job for two weeks to recover from something that a neurotypical brain would have snapped right back from. All three get along amazingly well, though they have had their misunderstandings which have sometimes been due to the typical lack of logic that is associated with having an FASD. There have been problems miscounting bank deposits, struggling to find systems that work better to keep things organized, and dealing with the fatigue that comes from working 10-12 hours a day which sometimes leads to miscommunications and memory issues due to exhaustion. They <u>are</u> working it out, finding ways to accommodate one another as well as their employees, and they are each thriving.

The hesitance I felt around homeschooling was real. The fears were valid and real. The enormity of the task was real. Embracing the desperation factor rather than fighting it was the key to phenomenal growth for both our children and me. It is important to note that we never would have been successful following a traditional path. In fact, we most certainly would have failed. The only way we were able to find our way was to recognize that we absolutely had to <u>think differently</u>; we had to acknowledge and embrace our limitations while also building on our strengths. We couldn't pretend there weren't significant delays and deficits nor could we deny that life would have to look different for them than for other young adults their age. But "different" isn't bad! There is no single right way to launch any of our kids, but we must ignore the cultural conditioning that continues to steer every learner toward college or relegates them to becoming the proverbial "burger flipper". Our kids can indeed be more if we can manage to widen our perspectives and accept the realities of what is, rather than what we wish it were.

What We Learned:

- With kids who have disabilities, too often we focus on what they cannot do versus what they can do.

Look at their strengths with as much vigor as you look at their weaknesses.

- Think big!! Self-employment is a growing area of real possibility for those with disabilities. There is a growing body of evidence that supports entrepreneurship for those who have disabilities because the work environment, schedule, and type of work can be adapted more easily than when a disabled person is employed by someone else.

    - https://www.dol.gov/agencies/odep/program-areas/employers/self-employment-entrepreneurship
    - https://www.ncsl.org/research/labor-and-employment/disability-employment-self-employment-and-entrepreneurship.aspx
    - https://www.easterseals.com/our-programs/employment-training/self-employment-people-with-disabilities.html

- Our kids are not the only ones who need support, parents also need support! Find individuals and groups where you can bring your whole self to the table, and where your current reality is not judged. Yes, this takes some real effort, but it is well worth it. If you can't find the right support, start a support group of your own, either online or in person. This is one of the most important things you can do for your child. Taking care of your needs as you walk a difficult road with them is what keeps the burden from feeling too heavy to carry.

- If you are not a natural researcher, find someone who cares enough about your child to help. This could be a friend, a family member, or even someone you know who is a "Master of Google" who you could pay to seek out resources for you to review. Sometimes simply knowing the best language to use when performing a search can yield remarkable resources. Even hiring a homeschool consultant may be a helpful option.

- Exude enthusiasm and the belief that your child can do anything he or she wants to accomplish. Build them up by gradually increasing the difficulty of tasks so they can see their progress. They need you as their cheerleader, but they also need to see their own progress. This progress needs to be pointed out in very concrete and specific ways, not generalized by saying things like, "But you are so smart!". Specifically, tell them where you saw improvement, where you saw a developmental leap and where you saw a gain (no matter how small). Small incremental steps still count as growth, but we often don't acknowledge those little gains the way we should, so we miss opportunities to celebrate.

Chapter 3

Natalie's Journey as a Homeschool Mom

"Mrs. Vecchione, we need you to come and pick up your son." Unfortunately, this was a phone call that I was used to receiving over the years and my heart would sink again with every call. Whether this call came from preschools, schools, camps, church events, or special activities....it was a call that I dreaded and I received on a regular basis. Most of the time, my getting this type of phone call was precipitated by a flare up of one of our son's many medical conditions or a sensory meltdown that could not be managed by teachers or staff. We would later learn that these medical conditions and sensory symptoms were all related to his having a Fetal Alcohol Spectrum Disorder (FASD), however these symptoms were often misinterpreted by teachers or staff as his being overdramatic about illness (he wasn't) or willful behaviors and "not being able to pull it together" (In having an FASD, his brain couldn't do that after being triggered in a stressful environment). As these calls increased in frequency, we discovered that we would be able to accommodate him best by homeschooling. Just like Cindy and her family, we began our journey as "Desperation Homeschoolers". Before we get into our homeschool journey, I'd like to share a little bit about our adoption journey, our family's journey with FASD, and how we ended up on a country road in the middle of the farm lands of rural North Carolina.

My husband, John, and I adopted both of our children through domestic adoption, however, our children each have **very** different adoption journeys. In 2002, John and I adopted our son, Nick, when he was 2 ½ weeks old and as soon as he was discharged from the hospital (where he was born in Reading, PA). Nick was born with quite a few medical conditions that required his hospitalization (which we later learned were a result of prenatal alcohol exposure and a lack of prenatal care). The day we met him was an incredible day, which was full of excitement and the nervousness of our being new parents. The staff in the pediatric unit at the hospital loved Nick and gave him the best care possible. To this day, we're still in touch with a few of the doctors and staff members on Facebook. Those staff members educated us about Nick's medical needs and how to care for our tiny, scrappy son. He even earned the nickname "Rocky", as he was (and he still is) a fighter!

      The early years of Nick's life were filled with specialists' appointments, medications, more appointments, and a realization in 2004 that Nick had been exposed to alcohol during his birth mother's pregnancy. During a follow up appointment from a sleep study, a pediatric neurologist shared with a group of medical students that he believed that Nick had Fetal Alcohol Exposure. That neurologist proceeded to tell those medical students what brought him to this conclusion. Stunned, my husband and I asked that neurologist "What should we do?" and the neurologist's nonchalant reply to us was "Oh, just put him in Early Intervention and he'll be fine." To this day, I still cringe when I think about that insensitive response. It also still saddens me, now as a parent advocate, that we were not given appropriate guidelines, support or even a written FASD diagnosis. Nick was placed in Early Intervention, but with a diagnosis of Sensory Processing Disorder. It would take 13 years after that initial realization to have a finally written confirmation of a FASD diagnosis for our son. Anytime new diagnoses arose, John and I asked "We were verbally told that Nick likely had prenatal alcohol exposure, could this diagnosis be a result of that?" to which, the answer was often a misguided "No"

As he grew older, Nick's symptoms increased in number, as did the list of his diagnoses. Due to the testing criteria for Early Intervention, Nick only qualified for one year, as he made sufficient progress for him to be taken off. However, new symptoms emerged and we often spent much time (and money) finding new specialists, tutors, and programs to help our son's needs. As a result of his physical, medical and developmental challenges, Nick was often the target of being bullied in elementary school. Even after switching schools on several occasions, other students continue to target Nick and the crisis of bullying followed him. Additionally, Nick spent much of his time on homework that he didn't understand. Due to his FASD-related memory deficits, Nick would be able to recall information on some days, but not on other days. He struggled with abstract concepts and cause and effect. On top of that, Nick's medical conditions started to become more problematic, which caused more time missed from school. By January 2014, Nick was missing so much school, that I eventually stopped working as a music therapist and began schooling him at home to make up for the schoolwork he was missing. Shortly before our official jump into homeschooling, I remember telling John, "You know, Nick understands these homework concepts better when I use different visual and kinesthetic strategies with him." John joked with me, "Maybe *you* should be his teacher." That statement would later become a reality.

Later in February 2014, while Nick was still sick at home, John and I attended what would be his last team meeting at his school. In the conference room, on that cold winter day, the principal, teachers and school psychologist listened to our requests for better accommodations, more time for schoolwork, and fewer or adapted homework assignments. Our requests were met with a chilling response, "We've done everything we are able to do; we are moving Nick to a completely inclusive, special needs track. We will provide him counseling so he can understand why he will not continue to be in the same class with his friends. We'll start this transition in the next few months." John and I were stunned. Even though Nick was struggling in some subjects, he excelled in others. While his reading, writing and math skills were not at grade level, he still managed to pass many of his quizzes and assignments. We thought we were not asking for much when we were asking for extra accommodations. Apparently, we thought wrong! After that meeting ended, one of Nick's teachers quietly pulled us into a hallway and in a hushed tone told us "Do ***not*** let him go into that program, you will lose the sweet boy that is Nick." To this day, John and I consider that former teacher to be an angel, as she confirmed what we already were thinking….the option presented to us in that meeting was not a good fit for our son and thus we were catapulted into beginning our journey into homeschooling.

    March 1, 2014 was our "official first day of homeschooling". I wish I could say we had a lot of fanfare or celebration, but it was a quiet day. Nick was still recovering from his acute, medical situations…so he spent most of the day on the couch and I taught him about Alexander Graham Bell (who was famously homeschooled). Having no prior homeschooling experience, I tried to recreate school at home (minus the desk and chair). Before I continue, please let me state for the record that homeschooling is **NOT** the same as "Schooling at Home", Virtual Schooling or the like. I also regret to say that we didn't spend any time "de-schooling", that is giving our son time to decompress from the stress of regular school. De-Schooling is a time period that is highly recommended in the homeschooling community, to allow children or teens a smoother transition from school to homeschool. Looking back after being a homeschool mom for more than seven years, I am convinced that Nick would have benefited from a de-schooling period to decompress, process the change and help with the shift to homeschool.

    Thankfully, I started to realize that homeschooling allowed us flexibility (for doctor appointments, therapy, tutoring) as well as opportunities to learn in more experiential ways. On the days that Nick was feeling up to it, we took field trips to museums, science centers, and historical landmarks. As the weather became warmer, we also did a lot of "outside school", giving us time for fresh air and exploring nature through hikes. I quickly learned that being active allowed for Nick's brain to process information in a more accessible way. For example, we practiced spelling words while he was riding his scooter and he recited math facts while riding his skateboard. Tapping into Nick's sensory-seeking behaviors and incorporating learning strategies into activities gave him the opportunity to better learn information. Astonishingly, I started using these techniques and strategies long before I learned about the science behind FASD and neurobehavioral parenting strategies.

    One of the *many* blessings of being a homeschool family is being able to take vacations that are not dictated by a traditional, school-year schedule. Once Nick was feeling better, we were able to see John's family in Florida <u>three</u> times in 18 months! Not only were we able to spend precious time with John's ailing father, but we were also able to take some wonderful field trips, beach trips and even work experiential learning into our Florida vacations (unbeknownst to Nick)! Having a homeschool schedule is SUCH a benefit, especially for families who need to or enjoy travel.

  Another blessing that resulted in 2015 was the adoption of our daughter, Gianna. John and I prayed and realized that my being home full time and homeschooling Nick was able to give us the opportunity to become parents again. We adopted our daughter (who is now 6) through an open adoption and we have a very close relationship with Gianna's birth mom. Her birth mom (who was a former flute student of mine) was also our son's babysitter when we lived in Pennsylvania. Our family is very close to our daughter's birth mom and birth mom's siblings…who were all adoptees themselves. John and I were BLESSED to be there for our daughter's birth and we have a good understanding about her birth mom's medical history. We are in communication with her birth mom on a regular basis and we cherish the relationship that we have with our daughter's birth mom and birth relatives. John keeps in touch with Gianna's birth father a couple of times a year. Our daughter and our son are almost 13 years apart - again, to say that their adoption journeys are different is an understatement! As parents of two children who are both adopted, John and I recognize and treasure the miracle of how God brought both Nick and Gianna into our lives.

  As precious and adorable as Gianna was as an infant, she also had colic…which meant little sleep during the summer and fall of 2015. In the late fall of 2015, Nick started exhibiting some concerning behavioral symptoms. At first, we thought he was "acting out" due to adjusting to life with a baby sister with colic. Things that John and I thought were willful or disrespectful "behaviors", actually turned out to be new symptoms of his undiagnosed FASD that were starting to come out in puberty. Puberty is a time when many **secondary behavioral symptoms** become more apparent, and this was especially disconcerting because we were still expecting Nick to "fit" into our old expectations. Some of these secondary behavioral symptoms include acting out, anxiety, low self-esteem, and self-harm. We were seeing all of these symptoms in Nick and it startled us. Specialist after specialist insisted that what we were seeing was a result of our family's new addition, decreased sleep, or that Nick was just "having hormonal changes". Whenever we brought up what the pediatric neurologist told us in 2004 about prenatal alcohol exposure, every doctor or specialist dismissed our concerns. At the time, the adolescent therapists and psychiatric practitioners that Nick was seeing would try new medications (which made things worse) or suggest therapy for Nick (which didn't help). As parents, we felt helpless watching Nick slowly descend into more secondary behavioral symptoms of FASD…while still not having a proper diagnosis or treatment.

      2016 brought many changes, as John took on a new job and we had an unplanned, but welcome move to a place special to both of us. John and I always had an affinity for North Carolina, as we met as undergraduate students at East Carolina University in the early 1990's, and we still had dear friends and loved ones in North Carolina. Although we knew moving to North Carolina would be a huge adjustment for Nick and our family, we also knew that our new state was very <u>homeschool friendly</u>. There were more opportunities for Nick to do the things he enjoyed, like dirt bike riding and being outdoors. John and I were hoping that having more enjoyable opportunities would help Nick through this tumultuous beginning of his adolescence. We even bought Nick his first dirt bike, to encourage him pursuing this more in his new community.

Although we had wonderful homeschool opportunities and great moments for our family, Nick's secondary symptoms continued to worsen. Thankfully, we met up with a wonderful FASD consultant, whom John had found while we were looking for a new psychiatric specialist for Nick. We are incredibly thankful for what we learned from this therapist and how our concerns were finally <u>validated</u> by someone who truly knew about Fetal Alcohol Spectrum Disorder. We were able to join an FASD Parent Support Group that became a lifeline for me. Once a month, I listened to other parents share their stories and experiences that were so <u>similar</u> to our family's journey.

During the summer of 2017, it became apparent that Nick's condition had become unstable and serious. As hard as his adolescent psychiatrist tried, Nick needed to be hospitalized for a co-morbid mental health diagnosis (90% of individuals with an FASD have a co-morbid mental health diagnosis*). His hospitalization was necessary, as he needed to be stabilized…but it broke me as a mom.

Nick had never been separated from us for more than a night or two and now he was an hour away from our home and John and I were only allowed to see him for one hour every evening. Parents would line up in the lobby to be approved and to receive visitor badges. It was surreal. The cafeteria, where the family visits were held, smelled of institutionalized food and commercial cleaner. On the first night of Nick's hospitalization, Nick didn't want to see us during his visiting hour, because he was furious that he had to be in a facility. He screamed at us and he couldn't understand why he had to be there. I went home from that encounter, and after we put Gianna to bed, I sobbed uncontrollably and curled into a fetal position on the floor of Nick's bedroom. For so many years, I prayed for change in Nick and what I thought were willful and disrespectful behaviors. Soon, we would learn something that would forever change my perspective of how we viewed our son's brain.

Hope came in the shadows of my brokenness. Every night, I fervently prayed what I knew was my "Broken Mama" prayer , Psalm 63-

> "Oh God, You are my God; Early will I seek You: My soul thirsts for You; My flesh longs for You in a dry and thirsty land where there is no water. So I have looked for You in the sanctuary, to see Your Power and Your Glory. Because Your lovingkindness is better than life, my lips will praise You. Thus I will bless You while I live; I will lift up my hands in Your name. My soul shall be satisfied as with marrow and fatness, And my mouth shall praise You with joyful lips. When I remember You on my bed, I meditate on You in the night watches. Because You have been my help, Therefore in the shadow of Your wings I will rejoice. My soul follows close behind You; Your right hand upholds me." - Psalm 63: 1-8 (NKJV)

As broken as I was, I had hope in my darkness that God was bringing our family through this season. I didn't know what the future held, but I knew Who held our son.

During Nick's hospitalization, we could tell which of the teens were new to the facility, as they would scream or cry at their parents in the cafeteria (the way Nick had) and beg their families to go home. Remarkably, we started to see more of the "old Nick" during the progression of his short but necessary hospitalization. Nick was always compliant with his medications and the strict rules of the hospital, which reassured John and me that he was trying hard to do what he needed to do to go home. With each visit, more of his personality emerged. Two nights before we would get the call that he was ready to be released, Nick even joked around with us. We were the only family laughing in the cafeteria. On the day before his discharge, I received another call that changed my life as a mom, but this call came with a surprise! The nurse on Nick's unit was giving me discharge instructions and follow up instructions for the next day. Although Nick still had a way to go, he was stable enough to be discharged and to go home. The nurse read me the instructions and recommendations for his follow up appointments. At the end of the call, she read me the list of diagnoses from his hospitalization. I was expecting almost all of the diagnoses…except for one. When the nurse said "Fetal Alcohol Syndrome", I almost fainted! Not only was Nick stabilized, but he was *finally* assessed for FASD and he actually met the criteria for Fetal Alcohol Syndrome! My hands trembled as I wrote down this new diagnosis that we long suspected, but had never had confirmed. Nick had a Fetal Alcohol Spectrum Disorder (FASD); it was acknowledged and we could now start the new journey that would accompany his diagnosis.

The months after Nick's hospitalization were tough, so I allowed plenty of time for decompression, rest, and starting new routines. Nick was interested in learning new skills with his hands and we started signing him up for introductory classes in trades, such as welding and forging. At the same time, John and I began mountains of paperwork for Nick to be on waitlists to receive services and support from the state. It became apparent that Nick's new diagnosis of FASD, and having a mental health diagnosis, would open new doors for him. Unfortunately, many others were also in line for these services and support, so we continued to receive the best support from other parents of kids with FASD and through the kindness of those people who genuinely wanted to help our son. Nick also began tutoring with an <u>amazing</u> tutor, who took the time to learn about FASD and helped Nick re-ignite the spark in learning in out-of-the-box ways!

A year after our move, we experienced alienation in the suburban neighborhood where we lived. Early that summer, prior to Nick's hospitalization, we called the police, as we feared that Nick was suicidal. The kindly officers were able to de-escalate Nick and calm the situation until we were able to determine next steps. Unfortunately, one of those police visits happened at 6 o'clock in the evening when many neighbors were getting home from work so they watched the situation unfolding from their front lawns. After the hospitalization and as things were starting to settle down, we noticed that all of the neighbors (except one fellow homeschool family) stopped waving "hello", talking to us, or even acknowledging us. We became *"that"* family. Someone in the neighborhood even reported Nick's occasional dirt bike riding in our fenced-in backyard (something that he had done many times previously without incident) to our HOA…even though it was a regular occurrence for loud, leaf blowers to begin at 8 am on weekdays. We realized that we needed to move where we could have property, room to grow, and most importantly, where we would all feel welcome. Moving was necessary yet again.

To quote our ECU friend (who was also our real estate agent), we had moved from a very "hot" real estate market in a lovely suburb of Raleigh to a very "cold" market of rural North Carolina, so it took some time for us to find our *funky farmhouse*. In 2018, we found a home that checked many of the boxes of our family's unique needs: property, a floorplan with an in-law suite for Nick, our bedrooms in the main house, several workshops, and most importantly….no HOA! This was the home that our family could grow into and make our own. This was also the home that featured a detached workshop we would be able to convert to a future tiny home for Nick, whenever he was ready for that transition. I'm happy to say we've been in our *funky farmhouse* for over three years now. We live on a country road with many farms and we have the loveliest neighbors who know about our family and Nick's needs and support us! We are truly blessed. (Recently, our daughter, Gianna, commented that she wanted us to start thinking about where we were going to put *her* tiny house when she is finished with homeschooling! It looks like we're not going anywhere….)

Once in our new home, Nick attended a ***wonderful*** program sponsored by the North Carolina nonprofit organization, Josh's Hope Foundation. The mission of this foundation is "to serve the residents of North Carolina, ages 18-35 who live with mental health conditions and/or struggle with a substance abuse disorder. Josh's Hope provides vocational skills, job preparedness, independent life skills and therapeutic supports customized to meet the individual needs of participants."** When Nick turned 16, he was eligible to participate in a two-week, day camp at Josh's Hope called "Climbing Hope" that introduces 16–24-year-old, transition-age young adults to a variety of activities, including teaching and training in the use of carpentry tools and completing several woodworking projects. John and I were amazed that Nick came home with beautiful woodworking pieces. The piece that would change our lives, and his, was the first cutting board that he made for me. I still have that gorgeous cutting board, mounted in our kitchen. I've never used it, as I consider it a work of art (our family joke now is if Nick makes me a cutting board, I have to let him know if it's for "show" or if I will actually use it). John and I are forever thankful for Josh's Hope, as they found something that we never realized…Nick has a gift for woodworking and carpentry. This totally changed our homeschooling trajectory. Now, we knew that the last couple of years Nick's homeschool experience needed to become <u>Homeschool Trade School</u>.

>*Pei J, Denys K, Hughes J, Rasmussen C. Mental health issues in fetal alcohol spectrum disorder. Journal of Mental Health. 2011;20(5):473-483

** You can visit the Josh's Hope Foundation website at https://www.joshshopefoundation.org/

Chapter 4

Homeschool Trade School

"Let the favor of the Lord our God be upon us, and establish the work of our hands upon us; yes, establish the work of our hands" – Psalm 90:17

From Natalie-

As I write this chapter of our family's journey, I never thought that I would be typing these words on the desk that our son built for us as our Christmas gift in 2019. When I walk around our "funky farmhouse", there are beautiful reminders in the craftsmanship of our son's carpentry and woodworking- a hand turned bowl, an original woodwork wall art piece, a keepsake jewelry box (crafted with my favorite exotic wood- Purpleheart) and many cutting boards. I treasure everything that both of our kids have made me, but Nick's woodwork pieces have added significance as visual reminders of *how far he has come in his journey.* Each piece tells a story of where he was in his journey as a carpentry and woodworking apprentice. Additionally, I love how much *I've learned* as the mom of a budding, young apprentice. I love learning about all types of wood, tools, machinery, plans, trends, and anything related to carpentry or woodworking. There are many perks in being the mom of a carpentry and woodworking apprentice. I'd like to share why we chose this path of apprenticeship in teaching our son his trade and how we did it, since John or I are neither carpenters nor woodworkers.

Once we realized Nick's gift and skills in woodworking and carpentry, we first considered the more conventional ways for him to learn this wonderful trade. He tried trade school, working in commercial workshops and even having placements through Vocational Rehabilitation. On paper, these looked like optimal opportunities for learning. However, none of those options were a ***good fit*** for Nick. Vocational programs and trade school environments generally are a hard fit for our teens and young adults with FASD and other Brain-Based Diagnoses. Overstimulating environments, being easily influenced by smoking, vaping, or any other substances on the site, and ***not being able to keep up at the class pace*** are all factors that can contribute to being a poor fit. We tried several different options before realizing that the <u>best</u> way that Nick would learn his trade was through an "old fashioned apprenticeship". We were blessed that Nick had not only one, but two, outstanding and kind apprenticeship teachers in Andrew and Will. Before I explain <u>how</u> our son learned his trade in "an old-fashioned, nontraditional way", I'd like to discuss how apprenticeships used to be ***the*** only way to learn a skill or trade.

By definition, an apprenticeship is "<u>an arrangement in which someone learns an art, trade or job under another</u>".* (Merriam-Webster Dictionary) The history of apprenticeship dates back to ancient times, when young people would be employed with a master craftsman, in exchange for room and board and formal training in their craft. The more <u>formal</u> system of apprenticeships really developed in Europe during the Middle Ages and soon were under the supervision of craft guilds, trade unions or town governments. In early America, apprenticeships were common during the colonial era and developed into a necessary part of craft and trade industries.** (Britannica.com) As the United States developed into a modernized and industrialized nation, the nature of apprenticeships changed from less of a *learning* experience to more of a *work experience*. Today, teens as young as 16 may begin formal apprenticeships as part of their education, and homeschooling made that a great option for Nick. However, since many trades require a high school diploma, most teens and young adults start their apprenticeships after graduation and/or through trade schools.

    When we met Andrew, Nick's first carpentry apprenticeship teacher, it was a difficult season for our family. Nick had finished a major, medication adjustment and his girlfriend (of over a year and a half) broke up with him. Our sweet son was feeling very broken. Andrew and his beautiful family came into our family through God's Orchestration. Andrew answered a Facebook Marketplace ad that I had placed, and he had made plans to come down to our home (about 45 minutes from his home) with his trailer to purchase a substantial amount of cedar we had for sale. An hour after he said he would be at our home; he still hadn't shown up. Frustrated, I was about to move on to the next potential buyer….but the Holy Spirit put me on pause and urged me to reach out to Andrew. Later that night, Andrew messaged me and apologized - his phone battery died, he had no GPS and he was on our farm-access road, but could not find our house. In Andrew's defense, our road is not well-marked and you really have to know where you're going since houses are nestled between farms. Once he arrived at our house, Andrew shared that he could only come during the night, since he cared for his young kids during the daytime and he worked at night in his independent business as a carpenter / woodworker. My heart softened and I definitely knew the Lord had placed Andrew in our lives for a reason. I shared a little bit of our family's journey and Nick's newfound love for carpentry and woodworking. Andrew shared a little of his journey as a Marine Vet who was acclimating to civilian life and coping and adjusting to life after sacrificing so much of his life as a soldier. Andrew shared that he would be interested in helping to teach Nick. Carpentry and woodworking had become therapeutic for Andrew and he knew this could also be the case for Nick. I encouraged Andrew to bring his trailer the following day and to bring his kids. I would watch the kids while Andrew loaded wood and he could spend time with Nick. (This would become a new routine that our family treasured for the next nine months.)

    The next day was filled with happy, unexpected surprises. When Andrew and his kids arrived, trailer in tow, his two young kids immediately connected and began playing with our daughter, Gianna. I explained to Andrew that Nick had had a rough night and he might or might not come out to meet him. (Sleep Difficulties are very common in individuals that have an FASD, especially when they are dysregulated). Andrew completely understood and I cautiously waited outside with Andrew and the kids to see if Nick would come out. Amazingly, not only did Nick come out, but he also introduced himself to Andrew. Andrew got their relationship off to a great start by giving Nick a hat from his carpentry business and inviting him to learn from him. This elicited a big smile from Nick, and that told me so much. Throughout his life, Nick would show glimmers of genuine happiness through his magnetic smile. During his teenage years and especially around his hospitalization (and our family getting our footing), his smile was elusive. Reflecting back on those years, we saw less and less of his magnetic smile…but not on the day Nick met Andrew. I remember how Nick smiled when he met his hero and how he learned that his new hero would be his first carpentry and woodworking teacher!

We started this new apprenticeship adventure with FASD Education for Andrew, I explained to Andrew how Nick's brain operates and how to break down instructions into simple, short directions. I even shared a copy of the book "Trying Differently Rather Than Harder" by Diane Malbin (the go-to book about Fetal Alcohol Spectrum Disorders). Although Andrew had never taught carpentry or woodworking to anyone, he had amazing skills and a natural ability. He genuinely wanted to help Nick and be a part of Nick's aspirations of learning carpentry and woodworking. Having a good knowledge of leadership from his service in the Marines, Andrew was attentive and utilized the shared FASD knowledge to teach Nick in the ways that were best suited for him. That September, we started a weekly routine of driving an hour (each way) to Andrew's home, where his workshop was located right next to his home. I would bring a giant bag full of activities, crafts, preschool worksheets, and surprises to teach and entertain Gianna and Andrew's two adorable kids inside while Andrew taught Nick and worked with him. During those months, our visits to see Andrew and his family were my favorite days of the week, since Gianna had fun with her new friends and Nick was enthralled with learning and building with his new teacher. We all left each visit to Andrew's home and workshop feeling happy and tired.

During that time, Andrew would also call Nick to help him with carpentry projects "in the field". Nick was able to assist Andrew with restoration projects and he even helped Andrew demo and build a new back porch for one of Andrew's customers. Nick quickly learned that as much as he loved creating in carpentry and woodworking, he equally loved *demo work*! Knowing what I do about the FASD brain now, this comes as no surprise! As a parent advocate in FASD, I'd like to explain the *why* behind that discovery.

One of the hallmark physical traits of FASD is in the area of Sensory Processing. Due to the brain damage from prenatal alcohol exposure, individuals with an FASD (or other brain-based diagnosis) can exhibit sensory processing challenges that can manifest in either *Sensory Seeking Symptoms or Sensory Avoidance Symptoms*. In the area of physical activity, Nick was always a "Sensory Seeker", especially when it came to proprioceptive activity. This meant that Nick needed to feel extra weight or pressure to help regulate him. John and I could recall how Nick sought heavy work or pressure from physical activity, throughout his young life, to fill those *sensory seeking needs.* Demolition work in carpentry, such as tearing down an old deck, breaking down walls or old structures was therapeutic for Nick. He was able to use his strength and sensory-seeking motivation to literally tear down walls and take out his frustrations. Demo days have always been a favorite for Nick, as they are also days of sensory input. Demolition literally regulates Nick.

Perhaps one of the most amazing gifts from Nick's time with Andrew was the connection that Nick and Andrew developed…they both experienced loss and trauma, and found ways to reinvent themselves through their woodworking and carpentry. Andrew came during a season of Nick's life when Nick was vulnerable, extremely depressed, and very unsure of himself. Andrew innately understood how Nick experienced the world in a different way. Even more, Andrew embraced Nick's differences and Nick's sense of humor. Andrew, the "hero sniper dream teacher" (as Nick would call him), was like the coolest big brother to Nick. Andrew was much younger than John and I, so Nick could relate to him in ways that he could not relate to John and me. Nick had the utmost respect and admiration for Andrew…yet at the same time, Nick would laugh hysterically at Andrew's antics in the workshop. It would make my heart smile when there was a lull inside, when I was playing with the "littles", and I could hear the sound of Andrew making Nick laugh in the workshop. One of the amazing gifts that comes with the experience of apprenticeship is the ability of the apprentice to bond, connect, and learn from his or her teacher. For many of our teens and young adults with FASD and other brain-based disabilities, that ability to connect and be mentored by a safe, responsible and caring adult is priceless. In addition to learning his craft, Nick learned life lessons from Andrew. Andrew was, and always will be, Nick's first mentor and for that John and I are eternally thankful to him.

> "To everything there is a season, A time for every purpose under heaven: A time to be born, And a time to die A time to plant, And a time to pluck what is planted; A time to kill, And a time to heal: A time to break down, And a time to build up…"
>
> – Ecclesiastes 3: 1-3

Just like all things, Nick's time with Andrew had to come to end. Andrew was finishing his Master's Degree and needed the time in the Spring to focus on his studies, so we tried a trade school program, which a family friend had suggested, and that literally lasted less than 24 hours. Instantly, we were reminded that *any* trade school option would not be a good fit for Nick as trade schools and trade school environments are not a good fit for many of our teens and young adults with an FASD (or other brain-based disability) for many reasons. In March 2019, we were back to square one. We needed to find a new carpentry and woodworking apprenticeship teacher with whom Nick could finish out his homeschool journey. The fit would need to be perfect, since Nick had an amazing apprenticeship experience with Andrew.

John and I prayed that the Lord would bring in an equally amazing apprenticeship teacher to teach Nick (and of course, the Lord SURPASSED our prayers!) How would that happen? As a "mama bear", I did what any mom of a teen with a diagnosis or disability would do! I researched, I advocated, I emailed, and I cold called over 50 local carpenters and woodworkers in our vicinity. I put together an introductory email explaining a little bit about our family, homeschooling, and Nick's journey. I shared enough, but not too much. What I especially wanted to communicate in these emails / phone call scripts was how Nick learned, his gifts, and how he could be an asset to the right carpenter / woodworker. Out of the fifty woodworkers and carpenters I contacted, four of them returned my calls or responded to my emails. Out of those four returned calls and emails, God's Orchestration placed Will, Nick's current apprenticeship teacher, in our lives.

Will's lovely wife, Annette, first received and read my email, which was filled with explanations and our hopes for finding Nick a new apprenticeship teacher. I still smile when I think of the first words Will said to me when he called me back to initially talk. Will said "My wife told me that the Lord is putting this young man into my life for a reason. How can I help him?" Instantly, I knew that Will would be Nick's new apprenticeship teacher. Will and Annette had just finished building their new home. During our phone call, Will shared that he was still putting together the final touches of his new workshop and Nick could even help him with that endeavor. Will also explained to me that his carpentry and woodworking business was his side business, so he was only available to teach Nick during some evenings and some Saturdays. This was absolutely fine with us! I asked Will if it would be OK if I educated him about FASD and how Nick learned and interacted differently with the world? Will agreed and he was happy to learn. We set up our first in person meeting on a cold, rainy evening during the first week of April 2019. It was just Nick and I going to meet Will. Will and Annette were closer in age to John and I, so Nick's interactions with Will would be different than his interactions with Andrew. During our ride to Will's workshop, I reminded Nick that being with Will would be a different experience, but I knew the Lord was putting Will in our lives for a great reason. Nick was nervous, but he agreed to meet Will and tour Will's new workshop.

Will welcomed us to his workshop with his kind demeanor and warm hospitality. Will had a very different personality than Andrew, and I wondered if that would make a difference to Nick? Thankfully, Nick felt very relaxed and enjoyed listening to Will tell him about his hopes for his unfinished workshop and the projects that he already had planned for the spring. Although a much different experience for Nick, this apprenticeship would be just as therapeutic and full of learning opportunities. We agreed that Nick would start out one evening a week and help Will finish setting up his workshop, building the cabinets in the workshop, and planning for future projects. One of my favorite sayings, that Will shared with us during our first meeting with him was "I'm looking forward to making sawdust with you." With those words, Nick began his apprenticeship with Will and he still apprentices with Will to this day.

Will understood that Nick learned best with fewer steps, concrete examples, and learning at Nick's own pace. In fact, Will taught Nick in a way that Nick thrived and which still surprises us! In a similar way to Andrew, Nick developed a bond with Will which built his confidence and nurtured his strengths. Additionally, Will's personality, love for music, and sharing funny stories would always *boost Nick's mood.* Nick would always leave Will's workshop in a much better mood than he entered and we joke that Will is Nick's "Vitamin W". Will <u>always</u> helps Nick get into a better mood, no matter how low Nick is feeling. Will also understood that Nick had quite a few medical conditions related to his FASD and Will has always been flexible in Nick having to reschedule or cancel if he wasn't feeling well.

When Will had occasional Saturday mornings when he needed extra help, Nick would almost always say "Yes!" As a result of Will's teaching, Nick's craftsmanship and skills as a woodworking and carpentry apprentice have dramatically improved. John and I are amazed by the projects made by Nick and Will! During Nick's last year of homeschool (prior to COVID19), Nick had the opportunity to be featured as a young woodworker for a Christmas Sale at our local art center. In between Will's projects, he would let Nick make cutting boards, hand-turned bowls, and trays to display for his show. That was a very busy couple of months and I don't remember exactly how many items Nick made (with Will's help), but I know that every one of them sold. Nick was proud that his work was highlighted and so many attendees were interested in *woodwork that he created.*

On a completely different note, Will and Nick also share a total aversion to spiders, especially ones found inside the workshop. I'm not sure if their mutual dislike of spiders strengthened their teacher / apprentice teacher/apprentice bond or just gave them more stories to discuss. To this day, spiders continue to be the mutual nemesis of Will and Nick. During the warmer months of the year, when I would go to pick up Nick, I would often find him and Will outside playing a game of cornhole on the porch of the workshop. On those evenings, I wondered if they had earlier found a spider inside the shop, but I just kept quiet and let them be….

Besides working in an amazing workshop with an incredible teacher, Nick was learning about subjects like math, physics, machinery, science, and business skills through his apprenticeship with Will. He would challenge Nick to cut and measure with increasing precision. Nick learned how to use "old school" methods for his lathe work, staining, and sealing projects. The beauty of a one-to-one apprenticeship allows the teacher to share "tips of the trade" and "old school methods" with his or her student.

An apprentice is not just learning his or her trade, but developing his or her own style in the craft or trade. Apprenticeships also allow the student to learn through "out of the box" experiences.

      Recently, Will invited Nick to go with him to pick up a fallen Black Walnut tree that was "gifted" to Will. The experience of going on a drive, learning about how to move a very large tree and the process of getting it to where it would be dried was an amazing learning opportunity for Nick! After a year, the Black Walnut would be turned into lumber for future projects for Will and Nick. Nick shared that he learned so much and he truly enjoyed what he learned that Saturday with Will. Even though Nick officially completed his homeschool last year, Nick continues to be Will's apprentice because ***learning doesn't stop when the homeschool journey is finished***. Will has shared with us that Nick can continue being his apprentice for as long as he is able to do so. Will (and his family) has blessed Nick and our family in countless ways. Perhaps the biggest blessing in Nick's apprenticeship is Will's genuine hope for Nick to be happy and his delight in helping Nick grow in his trade…and in life. In Will, Nick has found a teacher, mentor, and a good example of someone who embraces Nick for who he is, the amazing young adult that is our son.

What We Learned:

- Although trade school is a good option for many individuals, it may not be a good fit for those individuals with neurodiversity and especially with FASD. An alternative option, that is growing in popularity among the homeschool family, is taking trade classes through are nonprofit organizations and community centers. In North Carolina, "Shop Space" is a wonderful nonprofit organization that offers access to classes, tools, and space to help create a community that supports hands-on experiences in skilled trades. Nick actually participated in several forging and welding classes at Shop Space, in the beginning of his "teen homeschool years".
https://www.shopspace.org/

- Community and recreation centers may also offer introductory classes in skilled trades. Check with your local community or recreation center to see if such classes are available online or in-person (as COVID19 regulations permit).

- There are trade schools that are specifically for individuals with learning differences and developmental disabilities. You can research these schools on several websites including https://www.vocationaltraininghq.com/best-vocational-training-programs-disabled/

- Like Cindy previously stated, give your older kids / teens the opportunity to shadow, observe or volunteer with someone in a trade of their interest for a short amount of time. Prior to setting this up, speak or meet with the professional to explain the needs, accommodations, safety requirements and expectations for your homeschool student (preferably with the parent present). Check out to see if the environment is too overstimulating or overwhelming for your homeschool student. If it is, move onto the next place. Even if your kid / teen is observing for a short amount of time, you still want to make sure the environment will be a good fit for his or her needs.

- If you chose the route that we did and find a local tradesperson who is able to work with your teen's needs, learning differences, and sensory profile, then it's helpful to include the following in your preliminary contact email or letter: who you are, where you live, that your family is a homeschool family (read- *flexibility in scheduling*), your teen's age, your teen's diagnosis, and challenges that he or she may have in learning (offer to teach the potential instructor about your teen's diagnosis / needs), *your teen's gifts* (offer to provide letters of recommendation and/or examples of your teen's work, background about your teen and his / her interest in the particular trade or skill area, a little bit about their homeschool experience), and their limitations or needs (i.e. math, social / developmental dysmaturity, best strategies for learning, physical endurance, safety measures, etc.) Preparing a few, short "getting to know you visits", where you can stay and observe the potential "fit" of your teen with their prospective mentor or teacher will be extremely helpful.

- When possible, bring information and books to help them understand the needs of your teen. For both Andrew and Will, I provided a copy of "Trying Differently Rather Than Harder" by Diane Malbin, MSW and they both shared that knowing about FASD and how Nick processed and learned differently (and had memory deficits) was extremely helpful in how they both broke down tasks for Nick.

Chapter 5

Tips and Tools for Homeschooling Teens with Developmental Disabilities

From Cindy-

Visual Supports: We often forget the value of visual supports as kids mature, tending to relegate that sort of thing to the elementary school years. For those with developmental disabilities, the use of visual supports can be a true game changer! How do you do that for a more mature learner? Think of "Time" magazine…how many maps, graphics, and photos are used to explain their content? We all take in information visually, and your older learner will truly benefit from this sort of presentation, and in fact sometimes may struggle to comprehend more challenging topics without it.

Need ideas for how to do this effectively? Google photos of everything you talk about! Use maps faithfully, keeping a laminated one handy or a wall map front and center. iPads/tablets are superb for this purpose as the screen doesn't create a physical/psychological wall between you and your learner, and things can easily be shared by holding up the screen to show what you discovered. Are you studying a particular founding father? Display various photos of them. Learning about physical science? Find videos to illustrate various principles. Trying to explain what a political protest looks and feels like? Find images to share and watch videos of one.

Repetition, Repetition, Repetition! For struggling learners, repeating and reviewing information regularly is the key to retention. Always review every single lesson at the end of each learning session, and again the next day when you begin the next lesson. Review repeatedly, to the point of soul-killing for the educator!

How do you review? Don't just repeat what you taught the day before. Ask your learner what *they* can recall from your previous session. Don't jump in and give them the information, sit with them as they work on pulling it up from their memory. If they cannot come up with the answer to your questions on their own, encourage your student to look through their materials if needed, as that helps them learn the skill of researching and reflecting, and they will get better at that over time. Offer a key word or phrase and ask them to share what they remember about it, but don't fill in the blanks for them if they can't recall, direct them back to their resources to jog their memory.

See, Touch, Do If you keep this in mind, it will help more than you know! Repeat the phrase yourself until you have it embedded in your own brain, then look for every possible way to follow your personal mantra of "See, Touch, Do!" when teaching your kids. Bring in ways to learn that involve physical movement, art, music, etc. Find as many ways as possible to teach a particular point! Reading and discussing are not enough, nor is a hard and fast adherence to a particular "learning style" for a challenged student. Tackling a topic using as many modalities as possible allows the student to encounter the material in multiple ways, and that sort of repetition makes a difference.

For example, when teaching about the pioneers, have your learner read about it, watch a movie or documentary about pioneers, go to a museum to see old western covered wagons, build models, talk about what life would be like living in one and what would be hard. If possible, find someone to pull your kids around in a horse drawn cart or wagon so they gain a sense of what it would feel like to spend months traveling in one…the movement…the work involved with the horses, etc.

There are numerous ways to educate someone, and textbooks are only one way. The "See, Touch, Do!" process can also be used for more traditional high school subjects as well. When learning about United States Government, you could read about it, watch films that highlight the Supreme Court and an important case, interview local politicians, attend a local City Council meeting, draw charts reflecting the current names of people filling seats in the three branches of government, and view documentaries about important government officials. "See, Touch, Do!" engages as many parts of the brain as possible, and that alone increases retention!

Lapbooks or Notebooks: Usually reserved for the younger set, lapbooks or notebooks are great for older kids with FASD or developmental delays. Your learner works with materials in a different way, they craft and draw out key points in a visually appealing format, they discuss material with you as they do so, and they end up with a concrete product to refer back to.

Opinions: Everyone has an opinion; teens more than most of us! One great way to get far, far more writing practice out of your learner is to teach about a topic, then ask their opinion about it. Taking the pioneers above as an example, have your kids write by asking them, "If you were alive in the pioneer era, would you want to travel that far and take the risk? Or do you think it would be safer to remain where you were and develop a life there? Why?" or "What would be the thing you would hate the most about being a pioneer? What would you like the most?" For older kids you could ask, "Do you think the government handled the situation with Native Americans and Pioneers well? Why or why not? If you were the president at the time, how would you have handled the challenges of the interactions of those two groups?"

As you are sneaking in more writing practice, you need to remember one important thing when it is not "officially" for English class: DO NOT CORRECT THE WRITING!!! NO, NO, NO!! This is about working with words and thinking logically, building a framework to enjoy writing to share your thoughts, and developing critical thinking skills that are often lacking in kids who are not neurotypical. Good writing comes from good thinking, and kids with FASD need far more work with good thinking, logic, and reasoning. Discuss their opinions, but do NOT attack their opinions. Urge them to support their written statements.

I was shocked to discover that anytime I asked my kids not to answer a typical question, but instead to offer their opinion about something, they would often write far more than I would have required of them in order to prove how "right" they were. This method ultimately yielded high quality writers in the long run. In writing class, you can correct formal writing. The rest of the time, however, just get them writing and don't discourage them by uttering a single word correcting their punctuation, mechanics, etc. Opinion writing for a class other than English is for THINKING and offers the freedom to let ideas flow; not for writing practice. We can lose our learners' hearts when we pound too hard and correct too much.

Know When to Hold 'Em, and When to Fold 'Em:
When you find yourself continually asking, "Is this doing more harm than good at this stage?", you can pretty much bet it is, indeed, doing more harm than necessary. When you have hit a wall that is likely not going to be overcome, it is time to move on. Nothing demoralizes a student more than to continue pounding a subject area that their brain damage will not allow them to master. Often this is more about "educator ego" than the learner.

Our daughters, Olesya and Angela, truly struggled with math, as is typical for many teens with FASD. Olesya also has Dyscalculia and at 21 years old can still barely handle 4th grade math. Angela made it as far as Pre-Algebra but at that stage (and at 17 years old) it was clear we were maxing out her abilities as well. Rather than damage their spirits over something that was likely never going to change, we moved on to consumer math, business math, and using calculators. When a single subject challenges them deeply, learners will consider themselves "globally stupid". Recognizing the possibility of this transfer of their self-identity in considering themselves "less than" to "making accommodations" is life altering, if the parent is sensitive to it and willing to act to change course!

Shhh! Brains that are more distractible need a quiet learning environment with no distractions from dishwashers, the house phone, or the clothes dryer. Walls need to be less "busy" with less visual stimulation. Desks can distract as well, so keeping surfaces cleared as much as possible is very helpful. Absolutely no cell phones should be present when working on school work, no messages answered, etc. Exceptions can be made and phones MAY be used if a learner has self-control, as it might be handy to have the device handy to research visuals or topics being discussed. Having a hard and fast rule around cell phone usage can be important, but flexibility can be offered by having frequent breaks during which messages can be checked and responded. This includes the educator as well! Model the behavior you want your kids to exhibit. Do not allow yourself the distraction while teaching your kids!

Structure: Kids with FASD and those with other developmental delays thrive on structure and a schedule. For example, our schedule looked pretty structured as we sat down at 8:30 am at the table every single school day, ready to learn, tools in hand (pen, notebooks, textbooks, etc.), and dressed appropriately for the day. Lunch was at a fairly consistent time. The end of the school day was at a regular time, which was often dictated by volleyball practice. When the brain is stretching and challenged, routine can be so helpful!

How do you build in the flexibility that homeschoolers so enjoy? By making your weekly schedule a bit less structured. Take an entire midweek day off, take vacations more frequently, and if you were up very late the night before, then make an exception for the next morning to sleep in late and begin instruction a couple of hours later. Ultimately, holding to a reliable schedule will help kids, who struggle, succeed in their homeschooling journeys.

Engagement: In order to encourage greater engagement during school hours, switch up your day with great intent. Spending time learning from a single source for many hours a day, such as using only workbooks or textbooks, or even online learning, is death to engagement for teens with developmental delays. Using a variety of methods to learn and shifting after 30-45 minutes to an entirely new learning tool will help maintain your learner's attention and focus. An example of this would be: to discuss current events for twenty minutes to start your day as you also review the day's schedule and activities, then move on to learning from a textbook, then maybe watching a video or two online, transition after that to using a literature textbook or other reading material which involves discussion with the educator. Add in a math course online, then a science experiment, and you have an interactive day that provides the opportunity to "dip in and out" of a wide variety of learning modalities. You can do this with your entire day, selecting curriculum delivered in various formats, and you can also do this with a particular subject, mixing up interactive and passive presentations of the information around a given topic. This method, along with several short breaks, helps the learner feel as if the day is moving along at a nice pace rather than bogging down with the constant reading of a textbook or workbook regardless of subject.

Guided Reading: Reading side by side with your student throughout high school is one of the single best ways to not only enhance relationships, but also to continue to work on language and vocabulary development along with comprehension. For some reason, around 5th grade when a learner is proficient in reading, adults stop reading alongside them. Assumptions are made about what is being understood because a reader is usually functioning well enough to understand the key points of the story and their general comprehension might be decent. However, there is nothing better for development than stopping to explain new vocabulary words, modeling how to pronounce them, and asking critical-thinking questions to help a teen begin to think more logically and connect the dots. Oftentimes, an adult can add their own experiences and knowledge to flesh out or further explain the reading selection, increasing the foundational knowledge of the learner. Reading side-by-side well into the teens, even with GOOD readers, is critical!

What does this look like in practice? Stop reading and ask what they think something means with great regularity, or ask them to describe what they understand from the last page or two. Check in with them as you encounter higher level vocabulary and have them supply a definition so you don't "think" they know something but can make certain they do. Memory issues and brain scrambling means a learner thinks they understood something clearly but they are often way off base! Checking in is key. Tandem reading means the story moves along…the educator reads a couple paragraphs then the learner reads a couple. The learner must follow along when the adult reads. Stop and explain, stop and ask leading questions about what the student thinks will happen next, or how a character might feel, or even what your learner's opinion is about a particular experience you are reading about. <u>This is engaged reading</u>; it is active and not passive, and retention is far stronger when reading happens in this manner and don't hesitate to read more adult materials as your teen matures, even if the reading is difficult.

<u>Don't Rush:</u> Learning isn't a race, regardless of what our culture celebrates! Studies show that the majority of those amazing kids who attend college at 14 years old are no further along in life ten years later than any other learner. If your learner is struggling but still making progress, move as slowly as needed, carry textbooks over to the next year, stop as often as needed to explain. When your child is having bad brain days, put it aside and don't press it…there is always tomorrow! This is customized education, and that can be difficult to remember when friends are sharing all that their teens are doing, which AP classes they are taking, and how they are doing advanced calculus as a freshman in high school! Your learner desperately needs you to create a <u>safe space</u> for <u>their own learning pace</u> and to hold onto that! If you try to move too quickly through material, it ultimately wastes time anyway, as the retention drops, and your teen might be demoralized by feeling unable to cope well with the faster presentation of material.

Text Support: Auditory learning alone leads to very little retention, so make certain to provide text support for auditory books, provide visuals, and when possible, supply the text for lectures, etc.

Good Enough: Keep in mind your learner can still function well in the world even if they haven't mastered a five-paragraph essay or geometry. If they don't do traditional high school chemistry or biology, don't stop teaching science, instead teach science at a middle school level and work for retention of key concepts! If they can read at a 7th grade level and write a decent coherent letter or "how to" paragraph, they can likely function as well as many adults. Knowing what "good enough" looks like is important so you don't wear out your learner trying to force them to perform perfectly, which leads to tension in your relationship.

Look for Strengths: Teach to your teen's strengths and interests and you will get far more "buy in" as far as participation. Use interests to practice reading, writing, and math skills. If they are fascinated with video games, have them read books on the history of video games, write out an idea for a plot line for a fantasy game, look up statistics for the most popular games being played, and do the math to determine the difference in the number of various games sold. There are so many ways to capitalize on interests and strengths that can lead to more engaged learning and possible career opportunities as they explore those interests in unique ways. As in the example above, a teen may begin to realize they think like a video game writer and can perhaps design game plots, or write a blog that gets monetized, or create a YouTube channel to review games. Or maybe they simply improve as a reader and writer because they keep practicing that skill because they enjoy what they are learning. Regardless of the outcome, it all leads to a better educated young adult!

Chapter 6

"A-Ha!" Moments and Finding Support

From Cindy-

As we progressed further into homeschooling (and as I gradually came to know our kids and their learning strengths and weaknesses better), there were several moments of clarity that stand out as key factors in moving us forward. Like many parents of kids and teens with special needs, we spent years scratching our heads, trying to figure out why our kids couldn't learn the same way as other kids. Of course, I blamed myself, often feeling like I was somehow failing them or that I didn't have the skills to perceive what was actually going on with my kids. It was difficult to discern in those first years what challenges were specifically due to their backgrounds and what was a result of neurodiversity. The factors that complicated this discernment included the kids' having such complicated and varied backgrounds, including: institutional living, developmental delays, trauma, neglect, English language learning and experiential deprivation. Over time, they were able to gain a mastery of English. However, it became clear that there were unusual patterns and behavioral symptoms that simply couldn't be attributed solely to their backgrounds.

One of our first eye-opening moments was during a school IEP meeting when Kenny had been home and attending school for three years. His English was proficient and yet he still could not read. I was sitting around the table with six or seven professionals, trying to get something out of them other than "in time he will catch on". Suddenly, one of them looked at me with compassion and said, "Mrs.

LaJoy, perhaps you are expecting too much. Kenny has an IQ of 82 and maybe you are just expecting that he will perform as well as your other sons." I sat there, dumbfounded for a moment, not because of the IQ score (that was common knowledge), but by the fact that his score was being used *as an excuse* for why Kenny couldn't read. Slowly, I let my gaze fall on each one of them. Quietly, I asked, "So, be honest with me. Does Kenny strike you as a low IQ learner? If you didn't have those test results before you, would you be saying that to his mom? If you met him on the playground, would you assume that he had a low IQ? Does he present as someone who is slow or that lacks the capacity to learn?" The silence told me everything that I already knew to be true and no one in the room would look me in the eye. So, I continued, "There is something else wrong and you all know it. Kenny doesn't present as an individual with a low IQ at all. Aside from academic performance, he is sharp, quick thinking, bright in math that is numbers-based and not letter-based, and Kenny thinks abstractly in ways that individuals with low IQ's cannot achieve. If you don't know what is wrong with Kenny, just say so…but don't blame his score from his IQ test as the ONLY reason why our son can't learn." One teacher actually had the guts to look up and respond by saying, "You are right, I don't actually believe his IQ is an 82, but I can't figure out the problem with why he can't learn."

From that moment on, I realized that we were on our own if we were going to find any help for Kenny, as the professionals were indicating they were giving up and they had the test scores to prove that he "couldn't do it". Since the professionals had the documentation to back them up, it was clear that they would no longer continue trying to diagnose the various learning disabilities that troubled Kenny. Interestingly, it was only a year later when Kenny was working with a new speech and language pathologist (in a neighboring school district) that my gut feelings about Kenny's intellect were confirmed. She literally laughed out loud and said, "If this boy has a low IQ, I will eat my diploma! There is something wrong here…have you considered FASD as a possibility?" With that one question, we began to feel like we would find our answers.

    Our "A-Ha!" moments came with great regularity with all three of our kids. The sheer volume of repetition of basic information or schedules (or even what we were having for dinner that night) was a big clue that something was outside of the norm. The lack of logic was regularly on display. We had some of the most unusual answers offered in response to school questions, things that made no sense at all! Baking pans were thrown away in the trash, dishes were not put away where they belonged (despite a desire to do so), months of the year were not memorized correctly…and so much more. One major "A-Ha!" moment came when we attempted to teach our teens how to drive. It was incredibly difficult for our teens to keep the car in the lane, make a turn or even start the car and put it into gear. Our son Kenny never even attempted to learn how to drive and we were blessed by his wisdom and acceptance of that fact. He was unable to ride a bike or even an adult trike, let alone attempt to drive a car! However, we had hope for Angela and Olesya and we were surprised at the difficulty they had with the process of learning to drive. Three years later, they were finally proficient enough to obtain their driver's licenses, but not without damage having occurred in our own driveway with each of them backing into our other vehicles.

We also realized that our walk in the world was going to require a different way of thinking involved medical care after Kenny turned 18 years old. While Kenny was receiving care at Shriners Hospital for his bi-lateral cleft lip and palate, we were faced with the fact that certain policies and rules were not meant for young adults like Kenny. He was expected to answer medical questions on his own, and due to his brain scrambling information, he often gave incorrect answers that could have led to serious consequences for surgical procedures. We made sure we had the proper documentation on file with the hospital, which indicated that I held a Medical Power of Attorney for Kenny…but that didn't seem to make a difference. The hospital staff saw a bright young adult before them and refused to believe Kenny needed me with him at all times and essentially accused me of being a "helicopter parent". Despite Kenny's repeated requests to have me present, we were both made to feel as if we were somehow in the wrong- despite thorough explanations that Kenny had an FASD. At every visit, Kenny had to remind the staff that I was his medical advocate and that he wished for me to be present with every interaction, so that he stayed safe. Every time that happened, we were made to feel as if we had a relationship that was stifling his ability to mature (rather than it being an accommodation).

The fact that this happened at a medical facility, where his diagnosis was on file was maddening and uncomfortable for both of us. After one particularly awkward visit, during which I was treated particularly worse than usual for insisting that I had to be present while Kenny answered medical questions, Kenny and I had a long discussion. Kenny shared something with me that he had realized that day. Kenny said, "Mom, I need to speak up more firmly from now on. I am a man and I have a disability, but you always end up being treated badly because you speak up for what I need. Now it is my turn because I don't want you being treated like that; you are NOT a 'helicopter mom' and I need to make that clearer whenever I am banking or going to the doctor. It is hard enough for you to be my 'external brain' and I need to step it up and make sure you are treated with respect by being clear with professionals about what I need. This is going to be for a lifetime, so I might as well learn it now!" Wow! We parents are not the only ones who have "A-Ha!" moments.

Sadly, throughout our parenting and homeschooling journey, we have found little support for issues with our kids' learning disabilities and their FASD. There were no in-person support groups, no FASD experts in our area, no families who were experienced mentors. We were mostly alone as we muddled our way without anyone to guide us. At that time, Yahoo Groups and Facebook Groups were the only places where I was able to find others who were experiencing the same things with their kids. While these shared and common experiences were helpful, I needed more. I yearned for in-person connection with others who would deeply understand the unique "madness" that is experienced when caring for a loved one with an FASD (let alone caring for three kids with FASD). There was no one in our area who knew much about FASD. The few families, who had adopted their kids through international adoption (and we met in our town), were struggling in their own ways with their kids' presumed FASD. With our family being a few years older than their kids, we ended up being the support for them!

Ultimately, we were blessed with a terrific group of friends from church and although they may not have understood FASD, they stepped up for years to help tutor our kids, take them on field trips, and celebrate their accomplishments. Those closest to us listened, offered encouragement, and even provided significant financial support from time to time…when therapies and other needs were too expensive for us to handle. Even though our friends from church didn't have a deep understanding of our kids' unique needs or have experience with international adoptees, they stood beside us as we tried to find answers and prepare our kids for adulthood. God reached right into our home and we were wrapped in the love of Mary Loncar, Jane and Steve Nannestad, Lael Van Riper, Pat Idsardi, Janet Sims, and others who were determined not to let us sink. Years later, I continue to recognize that I have a lot to "pay forward" as God's Love was abundant at a time when our family needed it the most.

Chapter 7

Blazing New Trails

From Cindy-

What do you do when faced with circumstances that are understood by few people (and with little experience)? <u>You research, ask questions, explore options and NEVER GIVE UP!</u> Through our pre-adoption training, we had a vague sense of FASD, but we didn't thoroughly understand the nitty gritty so I worked to educate Dominick and me about FASD by sharing pertinent information that I gathered in the quest to learn. Writing a blog for over a decade and developing a bit of an audience, I discovered there were other adoptive parents who were as flummoxed as we were by our kids' unusual behavioral symptoms, memory challenges, and more. By openly sharing the quirks, foibles, grief, and celebrations of our daily life, I began to gently educate others about FASD and Reactive Attachment Disorder (RAD), with which our youngest son, Josh, was diagnosed when he was a year old.

Through my puzzled posts, which would outline the discovery of a new symptom, helpful suggestions from other parents (who were doing their own investigations of symptoms) would emerge. This forum that I created helped our family as much as it assisted other families! On a weekly basis, I heard from other parents who had questions about how to best work with their child, on a behavioral and academic basis. I was humbled that God used me to perhaps help or even save others from the kind of pain and doubt that we had experienced for years. I was supported in this by Dominick, as dinner was often interrupted by a phone call from a frantic parent, or I would come to bed extraordinarily late after spending an hour responding to an email or sharing resources. My husband knew that we were walking on a different path from many parents and he encouraged me in my desire to help alleviate a little of the pain that others were also feeling as they were navigating their way down these new paths. With a limited number of experts in the United States who were well-versed in FASD, we parents became our own online support group while sharing information of what worked (and what didn't work).

Blogging provided me the opportunity to share the hard-earned wisdom that I had gleaned. One of the key things that I shared with others was the importance of being open and honest in our family conversations with our kids about their adoption journeys and their learning disabilities. Many parents really struggle with finding the right words, the right moment, or the right strategy to share this sensitive information with their children. In my writings, I would describe the conversations with our kids in detail, being hopeful in modeling how to face these discussions with compassion and grace. Although I was concerned about sharing so much of our family's life with the world, I also felt a responsibility to write in a manner that was both open and honest.

Every time I considered shutting down my blog, I had almost immediate signs, which I interpreted as coming from God, that told me to continue and that my writing was making a difference. Anytime I was getting closer to discontinuing to write, the next day I would have a family in crisis reach out to me. I would also receive a grateful message or email from another mom who had finally gotten an appropriate diagnosis for her child and she felt like she was finally on the right track...all because of something that she had read in my blog. Our entire family knew this sort of sharing was helping others and we all realized our own pain and experiences were being used for a Higher Purpose. As our kids matured, they began to see how little information was available (and everything we were dealing with), so they gave me permission to share experiences so other parents and kids wouldn't suffer and learn from our experiences.

Through my conversations with others, I realized that we developed close relationships with our kids who had FASD, which was a big contrast with other families who mightily struggled with their own family dynamics. We blazed new trails by virtually eliminating many of the secondary characteristics suffered by those kids and teens with an FASD. As we shared earlier in our book, the primary characteristics experienced by those kids, teens and young adults with FASD are those symptoms that directly resulted from the brain damage caused by prenatal alcohol exposure. The secondary characteristics result from a lifetime of the environment being a poor fit, symptoms being misunderstood as willful behaviors, and being blamed for actions that are beyond that individual's control. In other words, those who are around the person with an FASD can actually aggravate and create more behavioral symptoms due to lack of understanding, compassion, accommodation, and grace offered to that individual. The invisible nature of the disability causes others to expect neurotypical behavior and being constantly judged leads to anger, acting out, substance abuse, and severing of relationships.

How did <u>we</u> lessen or avoid dealing with secondary characteristics? First of all, we knew our kids were trying their very best and we quickly accepted that they were going to struggle through no fault of their own. Once we realized that certain "behaviors" or actions were not at all intentional, we were able to be more compassionate and understanding and assist our kids in finding better strategies for success. We stopped being punitive and started making accommodations. We still had expectations and standards, but we always understood that our kids had the desire to be compliant, but on any given day they simply could not. Just as you would not blame a person with a visual impairment for spilling milk, how can it be fair to blame a person with the memory deficits inherent with an FASD for losing yet another jacket? We stopped the "Blame Game" and instead shifted to becoming the "Support Fort". Our home was the one place where everyone understood how hard our three kids with FASD were trying, and it was also the one place where they could turn for suggestions and assistance when life was confusing or difficult. Their siblings, Matt and Josh, were an enormous help in this area! I have never met two more compassionate and patient young men. Even at very young ages, they were always kind, understanding, and supportive as we all learned how to best navigate life with an incredibly difficult disability.

Secondly, we laughed…A LOT…at everything! Our family used humor to diffuse painful moments and we giggled at the silly things that happened when a brain misfired. We <u>never</u> laughed at someone, but we did allow ourselves to be amused by yet another ridiculous misunderstanding. Instead of Kenny being discouraged by trying to make fudge and ruining it twice, we made a joke of it and turned it into a challenge. I quickly ran down to the store and bought enough ingredients for three more attempts, brought them home, and plopped them on the table. I told him, "Dude, you are going to succeed at making fudge if I have to buy every bag of chocolate chips in town! Keep trying!" Then, off he went, encouraged and willing to try again as we all laughed at the chaos in the kitchen from multiple batches gone awry. Olesya had a favorite and quite apt phrase for our entire family. When someone was having a bad moment, she would look up and declare, "That's OK, we're not stupid, we're just uniquely developed!" and we would all laugh.

Perhaps the best thing we ever did to minimize and avoid secondary characteristics was to recognize that the person whose brain was impacted by an FASD, was not a "bad guy". Our family members with FASD were just as upset, frustrated and, at times, as angry as the rest of the family! My favorite saying is, "Words mean things", which I use many times with our kids to help them understand the power of the language we use to help or harm others. Recognizing the truth of this, I would shift a particular situation by focusing that they were people with brains that worked differently. If we were having a particularly bad day with schoolwork or it was just one of those days when their brain was misfiring all over the place (and the tears were threatening to fall), I would clasp their hands in mine and boldly state, "I don't know about you, but I am SO frustrated with your brain today and I bet you are, too! When your brain doesn't want to cooperate, aren't you just sick of it?! It's you and me tag-teaming your brain and we're going to overcome this no matter what!!" That single tactic probably saved my relationship with our kids and it also allowed them to continue to retain their self-esteem in those painful moments. Doing this focused on them as individuals, with a brain that was not cooperating at the moment and placed both parent and child in the role of overcomer and not the perpetrator!

With Buckaroos Slices and Scoops, we were definitely trail blazers and we knew we would be from the moment we conceived the project. Though there was an occasional, national news story about a business that hired individuals with disabilities, there were few that we could look to as a model. Once again, desperation created aspiration and we forged ahead with a really big plan…one that most thought was inconceivable when considering the level of disability involved. We knew it was highly unlikely our kids would be able to maintain traditional employment, so we set out to create something that would accommodate their special needs and also would support further growth for them and for others. Financially, we put a lot on the line and our three young adults with FASD were quite serious about this venture. By doing so, we signaled to them how much we *believed in them* and they rose to the challenge. Self-employment is a great solution for those who struggle, but it can be a very frightening proposition when it's first being considered by an individual and their family. Having no guidebook to follow, we are continuously making it up as we go along….but so far, the results have been well-worth wading through the fear. We have spoken to many others, who are seeing self-employment as a possibility for their own family member(s) and they are eager to learn more.

Chapter 8

Embracing Interdependence

From Cindy and Natalie –

Letting go of prior notions of what it means to be an adult is a not an easy task. It can involve grieving the loss of the future you envisioned, when you first held your child in your arms. It certainly requires us to set our own egos and bragging rights aside as we embrace the young adult before us, releasing the dream of the young adult we once dreamed envisioned them to be. The future will indeed look different as you shift your thinking from independence to <u>interdependence.</u>

In order to shift your young adult toward acceptance of interdependence, it is imperative that you begin having conversations with them as young as possible about the likelihood of them needing ongoing support as they become adults. Doing this in a way that is still encouraging and filled with possibilities isn't easy, but once again, presenting yourself as a team working towards a common goal can be a helpful approach. You and your young adult are in a collaborative process as you consider options for their future. Together, you will discuss the support they might need, their strengths and what opportunities are available to them.

Moving through the teen years, observe your child carefully. Do they have the capacity to cook simple meals on their own with no assistance? Are they handling finances appropriately? Can they perform basic household cleaning tasks and maintenance? Are they able to develop their own social life outside the family, and are they making good choices? Every person with FASD has both skills and deficits. In order to make the best possible choices for their future, **_knowing your young adult is crucial_** in evaluating what level of support they will need, where the pitfalls are likely to be, and where they may excel. Keep in mind, however, that even the highest functioning adults with FASD often still need some form of support. Those who are more seriously impacted by FASD may need constant one-on-one care to ensure their safety. Since FASD is a spectrum diagnosis, no two FASD individuals will be exactly alike, so this process of evaluation will help you assess the specific areas of concern.

You may find that you understand the need for interdependence while your young adult rejects it. This is natural, as they want to move into the world without restraints (especially when they see their peers starting to launch). The teen years can be especially painful, as your child becomes more fully aware of all they cannot do compared to their friends, and they may desperately want to fit in. We all know this leads to risk-taking behaviors, and a seemingly inevitable decline can occur during this time. The desire to belong, paired with a brain that lacks critical thinking skills, is a terrible combination and can begin a downward spiral that ends in complete lack of relationship, poor life choices, addiction, and even premature death.

Individuals with FASD learn best by doing, so lectures are of little use. In the younger years, having your child begin to work on general "adulting" tasks around the house can lead to easing into tough conversations. In struggling with common household tasks, teens eventually come to certain conclusions themselves around their need for support. Examples of this may be: when they are in the mid-teen years and cannot easily follow a recipe, remember to turn the stove off, needing step-by-step instructions in order to clean their bedroom effectively or when they can't manage all the skills necessary to drive. As this happens, they will begin to internalize the need for ongoing support at some level in adulthood (without you having to point it out). Ultimately, this realization leads to their *not* thinking you are the one who is holding them back from "growing up".

Your goal is to help your maturing teen come to a place of acceptance around interdependence, but also to help them see how they are people others will rely on as well! Interdependence is a two-way street and explaining the reciprocity of interdependence is one key to acceptance. For example, point out how your knees aren't what they used to be, and how you need help regularly cleaning showers and tubs, or share with them that you will be happy to have their presence in your home longer than many parents get to enjoy their kids. Make sure to tell them how glad you are that you can count on them and you might need more help as you age! Use the word ***interdependence*** often and direct their attention to multi-generational families, who happily cohabitate and how all sides benefit from a lower cost of living, companionship, and by sharing the workload of maintaining a household.

Another concern of young people who have neurodiversity is they may feel that they will be a burden on their parents or other family members. They want to make their own way in the world, just like any other young adult. This emphasizes the need for your young adult to find some sort of meaningful work, even if in a sheltered setting, so that they might be able to contribute to the household as well as have a social circle outside of the home.

Some adults with FASD possibly are able to manage living alone, or with a roommate. However, they may still need assistance at times for such things as understanding medical or financial information, organizing meals for the week, or creating and following through with a cleaning routine for themselves or their home. Some families handle this by: creating an onsite apartment over a garage, adding on to their home to create separate living quarters, lining up support staff to visit the young adult. Weekly visits from support staff can help to assess where assistance is needed and provide it so that mom and dad can continue to be parents and not just caretakers. The decision on how best to achieve interdependence will vary from family to family, and from person to person, based upon level of disability and quality of relationship. For some families, the relationship may be too fractured to be able to be directly involved, but that doesn't mean the need for interdependence doesn't still exist. It means the interdependence extends to an agency and staff, and sometimes that can be the best possible solution for all parties involved.

Another thing to keep in mind when discussing interdependence with your young adult is to share current statistics, as the economy has changed the landscape of families and living situations. More families are living intergenerationally than have in years past. It is more common for people well into their forties to reside at home, with or without having a disability.

Many parents see that their kids who are impacted by cognitive and developmental delays are vulnerable in ways others aren't, and this leads many to ask if they should apply for legal guardianship or secure a Power of Attorney for their kids. This is a highly personal decision and is fully dependent upon the capacity of the person involved. Finding an experienced attorney, who specializes in working with families who have kids with disabilities, can be the best route to ensure you are making the wisest decision for your young adult. Involve your teen in these conversations and appointments, let their thoughts be heard, and be sure to compliment them on their wisdom as they contribute to the conversation. When framed appropriately, this does not have to be a situation that brings about despair. Presented as the way proactive adults take care of business, sharing how many adults have a power of attorney in place to protect their wishes if they can't make decisions, and empowering your young adult by asking them to participate in all phases of the planning is showing them the respect they deserve, and it also sends them the message that, though they may have a disability, you know they are moving into adulthood and are capable in many ways of making their own decisions. It is an act that honors who they are, not negates it, and it is important to treat it as such.

The most difficult part of embracing interdependence falls to the parent, for it can be a real challenge to shift your thinking and view your child who struggles so much as a "real" adult. Developmental delays and dysmaturity mean you may see an individual present in closer to his or her chronological age on one day and half of his or her chronological age on the next day. However, if interdependence is going to work, it is essential that you always respect the full-grown adult that stands before you. Though your young adult may still love watching SpongeBob cartoons (and may even enjoy playing with Legos at 19 years old) they are still an adult and yearn to be treated like an adult. Remember the accommodations that your young adult will need and to be implemented. In order to encourage a sense of interdependence and a willingness to allow you to intervene in their adult lives, you absolutely must respect their adulthood as much as possible…while providing the necessary support and accommodations needed for interdependence.

Chapter 9

Reflections for the Weary Homeschool Parent

From Cindy and Natalie –

> "Comparison is the thief of joy."
> – Theodore Roosevelt

How difficult it is to stop comparing your child to others and start enjoying the child you have! Your child was uniquely and wonderfully made, yes, not in spite of their disabilities, but including them! Homeschooling a child who struggles with academics means we parents have to hold tightly to our own self-worth, and we have to guard against looking to others or solely at our kids' achievement for our own validation. We can do irreparable harm to our kids if they sense we are disappointed in their performance, and we become disappointed when too much of our own sense of self-worth rides on the coattails of our kids' academic achievement. If you are homeschooling to provide your child with the kind of education uniquely structured to their needs, and you are accomplishing this, then you are successful. Even if you always move forward at a slower pace than others, you are still making progress and you are successful.

<u>Don't let the difficult road stop you from truly seeing and enjoying your child for who they are… God's beautiful creation!</u> When we make it all about the progress, we then fail to enjoy the journey, and our kids are lovely, resilient human beings. Delight in them! Do NOT turn them into your enemy. They didn't ask to be born with their disability, they are not at fault, and they are immature and often lack the capacity to dig deep when overwhelmed, or to fight through their own discouragement. Be your kids'

biggest cheerleader; it will pay off in ways you may never imagine.

<u>Education is not, nor should it ever be, a competitive sport or a race.</u> Consider homeschooling your learner past the age of 18 if you need more time to shore up fundamentals. So much brain maturation occurs between the ages of 18 and 21 (the kind that usually happens for most kids between the ages of 15-17 years old) that you can miss critical opportunities to cement previously difficult concepts which are easier to comprehend as the brain develops. So often, families homeschooling young adults with FASD graduate their learner at 18 years old and miss the opportunity to continue working with them just at the point when their development takes them to the next level where real gains would be realized.

There are times when your child needs to hear you fiercely say, "You are going it make it if it is the last thing we do! You are NOT going to end up a statistic and I KNOW IT for sure!" They need to hear you express certainty in their unknown and scary future! You need to speak into their lives, not just truth, but hope and the conviction that you believe in them. If all a learner hears is how you are fearful for them, or you continually point out how their brains don't function well, then you are locking them into an internal sense of doom. Your positive affirmations of a future that can be happy, healthy, and whole along with explanations of the odds stacked against them makes it clear that the reality might be difficult, and you are not denying that, but even so you still have confidence in their ability to overcome any obstacles. Say it loudly and say it often enough for them to take it in at a deep level.

You are so tired, so utterly exhausted, and there are days you are ready to give up. Your child is taking forever to learn some simple tasks, every subject is difficult, and you are at your wit's end because you don't have a clue what to do next.

STOP. Take a deep breath. Grab a piece of paper and a cup of coffee, and then make a couple of lists. Write down all the details about how far your child has come academically, all they have learned already even when it was so hard. Name every simple skill, every task they know how to do around the house, every surprising vocabulary word that you hadn't known they had learned. Next, make a second list, and on this list, you write down all the qualities about your child that you adore and admire, the little moments that brought a lump to your throat, the parts of your child that have nothing to do with schoolwork and everything to do with character.

Take that list and re-read it. See how far you both have come. See all that your child is beyond a grade. Say a little prayer of gratitude that you have made it this far, that you are continuing to make progress in little increments, and that you have been blessed to be the parent, nurturer, and protector of this precious heart. Afterwards, go hang out with your kid, play a game, watch a movie, remind yourself that tomorrow is a new day, and you will greet it with gusto and try again. Will this fix it all? No, but it might refresh your perspective just a bit.

Little gains add up, and for many kids, a mere 5% increase in function in even a couple of areas might mean the difference between full reliance on others or partial independence. Don't disregard the small successes. Over the course of their childhood and early adulthood, they add up to far more than you might realize in any given moment.

<u>Don't go it alone. Don't be embarrassed or ashamed to admit you are struggling.</u> God knocks on our door but doesn't bust His way in! Invite God into your circumstances by sharing your heartache with others, by asking for help from others, by being vulnerable enough to open up and accept the love offered by others in various forms. God loves us through others, God provides us with the support and encouragement we need through the kindness of those around us. When we are too uncomfortable to share our discouragement, we stop the flow of God's love into our life in the form of others. Be open, be honest, be courageous in sharing.

<u>We have walked the road you are on.</u> We have cried the same kind of tears, we have held all the same fears, and we made it to the other side. There are plenty of stories of broken families due to FASD, but too few stories of wholehearted, connected families that made it through. Those families…families like ours…are out there but they are quieter and they tend to fly below the radar because they are not in crisis. Look for others, learn from those who have gone before whose kids arrived at adulthood intact. Listen to the things they share…and don't shake your head and say, "That's impossible, they don't know MY kid!". We aren't magical, perfect parents, but we have tried a few methods that worked well. Give it a shot, no matter how little confidence you have in what we have shared. You might be surprised! All is not lost though it might feel like it right now, broken families can heal, broken relationships can mend.

Chapter 10 –

Moving Forward

From Natalie-

Cindy and I are so thankful that you have taken the time to listen to our stories and learn how we respectively blazed new homeschool trails for our families. We both truly wanted to share our stories so that you could use our lived experiences as inspiration in creating homeschool experiences for your families that focus on ***the gifts and strengths*** of your child / teen / young adult who learns differently. Cindy and I hope to be a resource, through this book, and through our future endeavors for the homeschool community.

Here are some questions that we would like to ask, to help you determine the next steps in your family's homeschool journey:

- Why do I want to homeschool my child? (if you're not a homeschool family)

- Why do I want to continue to homeschool my child?

- What is your vision for your homeschooling journey?

- What challenges or issues do I hope to address through homeschooling?

- What is the desired outcome of our family's homeschool journey?

- Who or what supports do I have in homeschooling my differently-abled child / teen / young adult?

- Do I have a regular opportunity for **Respite** and **Renewal**? (Note from Natalie- this is KEY for you!)

- How will we incorporate therapies (Speech, Occupational Therapy, etc.) or extra supports (tutoring) into our homeschooling schedule?

- Will our school district or county continue to provide services when we begin to homeschool (it varies from state to state and even county to county)?

- Are there Homeschool Resource Centers or Homeschool Support Organizations in our vicinity?

- What resources (local, state or national) do I have to help in our family's homeschool journey?

- Does my child / our family need time to decompress or de-school before we start?

- How can we configure a designated space for homeschooling or homeschooling supplies / books / activities / etc.?

- Is there a curriculum that would work best with my child / children?

- Are there resources for me to "outsource" some of my child's education (i.e., a tutor, mentor or specialized instructor)?

- What schedule would work best for my family?

- How can we connect with other homeschool families in our area?

- How can we incorporate field trips and plenty of opportunities for experiential learning?

- How can we make learning fun for our kids?

- What are my next steps?

We both HIGHLY recommend that prior to starting your homeschool journey (or as a reminder for those of you already homeschooling) that you ALWAYS make sure that your family can be / is in compliance with your state or province's <u>homeschool laws and regulations.</u>
Some questions you will need to address in being in compliance with your state or province's homeschool laws:

- What are the homeschool laws for my state / province?

- How can I access information to the homeschool laws / regulations for my state or province?

- If we are currently homeschooling, what are the requirements for withdrawing my child or children from school?

- Do I need to register our homeschool?

- Do I need to track attendance?

- Do I need to conduct annual testing? If so, what are the testing requirements?

- Do I need to provide my county / state / province with any additional documentation or reports throughout the homeschool year?

- What do I do if I am contacted by my local district or county with homeschool questions?

Cindy and I have both benefited from membership with the Home School Legal Defense Association (HSLDA). HSLDA provides answers to the above membership, plus assisting members if there are any questions or legal matters regarding your homeschooling needs. HSLDA also has a "Special Needs'' department to assist parents of students with any diagnosis or disability. https://www.hslda.org (Note- this is an unpaid endorsement; we are sharing our lived experiences as homeschoolers who have been members of HSLDA).

Finally, it is so exciting to know that there are so many families out there who want to create new paths and new homeschool experiences for their kids / teens / young adults who learn and interact with the world in different ways. Cindy and I have been blessed to create new paths for our (now) young adults that we hope and pray will give them a sense of fulfillment and accomplishment. We know that everyone has a gift, strength, or skill inside of them. As homeschool parents, we accept the privilege and responsibility that comes with discovering our kids' gifts, even when it means we're blazing new homeschool trails along the way!

For a limited time, you can get a free "Blazing New Homeschool Trails" companion journal!

For more information visit:
https://www.blazingnewhomeschooltrails.com

Made in the USA
Middletown, DE
25 August 2021